YOUR FAITH HAS SAVED YOU

Homilies for Liturgical Year C
Sundays, Solemnities, and Some Feasts

Rev. John P. Cush, STD

En Route Books and Media, LLC
Saint Louis, MO

⊕ENROUTE
Make the time

En Route Books and Media, LLC

5705 Rhodes Avenue

St. Louis, MO 63109

Contact us at contactus@enroutebooksandmedia.com

Cover Credit: Giorgio Vasari (1511–1574),
"St Luke Painting the Virgin," circa after 1565
Copyright 2024 Rev. John P. Cush, STD

ISBN-13: 979-8-88870-319-9
Library of Congress Control Number: 2025930345

Dedication

To the kind parishioners of the following parishes:

Saint Helen, Howard Beach, New York
Saint Bartholomew, Elmhurst, New York
Saint Saviour, Brooklyn, New York
Immaculate Heart of Mary, Brooklyn, New York
Saint John the Baptist-Most Holy Trinity-Saint Ann, Yonkers,
New York

who had to sit through all these homilies.

Table of Contents

Introduction

The Christology of the Gospel of Saint Luke

The Gospel of Luke, which we proclaim in the lectionary in liturgical year "C," offers a rich tapestry of Christological insight, portraying Jesus as the compassionate Savior, the fulfillment of God's promises, and the universal Redeemer. Through its narrative and theological framework, Luke reveals Jesus' identity, mission, and destiny in profound ways, emphasizing His role as the Son of God and the Son of Man, who brings salvation to all.

Who was the Evangelist Luke, the author of the Gospel we proclaim this liturgical year? The Gospel of Luke is traditionally attributed to Luke the Evangelist, a companion of Saint Paul and a physician by profession (Colossians 4:14). Luke was likely a Gentile convert to Christianity, which may explain his emphasis on Jesus' mission to all people, not just Israel. His background as a physician is reflected in the Gospel's compassionate tone and attention to human suffering.

Scholars generally date Luke's Gospel to circa 70–85 AD, placing it after the destruction of the Temple in Jerusalem. It was likely composed in a Hellenistic city, perhaps Antioch or another prominent center of early Christianity.

Luke explicitly addresses his Gospel to Theophilus (Luke 1:1-4), a name meaning "lover of God," which may refer to an individual or a symbolic representation of all believers. The Gospel was written primarily for Gentile Christians, evidenced by its frequent explanations of Jewish customs and its focus on Jesus' outreach to non-Jews.

Luke aims to provide a well-ordered and reliable account of Jesus' life to strengthen the faith of his audience. He writes, *"I too have decided, after investigating everything accurately anew, to write it down in an orderly sequence for you, most excellent Theophilus, so that you may realize the certainty of the teachings you have received"* (Luke 1:3-4).

The Gospel of Luke can be broken into three main sections: first, the Infancy Narratives (Chapters 1–2). This infancy narrative is unique to Luke, including stories not included in the narrative of Matthew's Gospel. These chapters include the Annunciation, the Visitation, and the Nativity. They emphasize God's intervention in history through Mary and highlight the joy and hope of salvation. Luke has a different emphasis than Matthew, which was written primarily for Jewish converts to Christianity and portrays Jesus as the fulfillment of the Old Testament more explicitly than the other three Gospels.

The second section details Jesus' Ministry in Galilee (Chapters 3–9). These chapters focus on Jesus' teachings, miracles, and the calling of His disciples. It portrays Jesus as a prophet and healer, filled with the Holy Spirit.

The final section of Luke tells of Our Lord Jesus' journey to Jerusalem and Passion (Chapters 10–24). Jesus' journey to Jerusalem, symbolizing His obedience to the Father's will. The Passion and Resurrection narratives emphasize mercy, forgiveness, and the fulfillment of Scripture.

Luke begins his Gospel with a Christological proclamation: the angel's announcement to Mary in the Annunciation. The angel declares, *"He will be great and will be called the Son of the Most High, and the Lord God will give him the throne of his father David"* (Luke 1:32). From the outset, Luke presents Jesus as the fulfillment of the Davidic covenant (2 Samuel 7:16) and the embodiment of divine sonship. His genealogy (Luke 3:23-38), tracing Jesus to Adam, underscores His universal mission as the Redeemer of all humanity, not only of Israel. The infancy narratives, particularly the *Nunc Dimittis* of Simeon (Luke 2:29-32), highlight Jesus as *"a light for revelation to the Gentiles and the glory of your people Israel."* This dual role underscores Luke's universal vision of Christ's salvific mission.

The Church Fathers discerned in Luke's Gospel a profound Christological depth. Saint Irenaeus of Lyons, in *Against Heresies*, emphasized Luke's portrayal of Jesus as the one who recapitulates humanity's story, restoring what was lost in Adam: *"He became what we are, that He might bring us to be even what He is Himself."*

Saint Ambrose, in his commentary on Luke, highlights Jesus' compassion and humility, particularly in the parables unique to Luke: *"In the parable of the prodigal son, we see the heart of Christ: a mercy that seeks not vengeance but restoration."* The Fathers often emphasized Luke's depiction of Jesus as the merciful physician, drawn from His statement: *"Those who are well do not need a physician, but the sick do. I have not come to call the righteous to repentance but sinners"* (Luke 5:31-32).

Saint Thomas Aquinas, in the *Catena Aurea*, collects the interpretations of the Fathers and highlights Luke's emphasis on the humanity of Christ. Aquinas notes that Luke's Gospel often presents Jesus in prayer, particularly before significant moments like His baptism (Luke 3:21), the choosing of the Twelve (Luke 6:12), and His transfiguration (Luke 9:28): *"In these prayers, we see the true humanity of Christ, who, though divine, sought communion with the Father as an example for us."*

Other Medieval commentators also reflected on Luke's title for Jesus, *Kyrios* (Lord), a term that appears frequently and underscores His divine authority. They linked this title with the Resurrection appearances in Luke, where Jesus is proclaimed as the victorious Lord of life and death (Luke 24:34).

Modern scholars and theologians have deepened our understanding of Luke's Christology by emphasizing its narrative theology and social dimensions. Hans Urs von Balthasar highlights the "kenotic" Christ of Luke, particularly in the Passion narrative: *"Luke portrays Christ as the suffering servant who freely embraces His destiny, offering Himself for humanity in perfect obedience to the Father."*

Pope Benedict XVI, in *Jesus of Nazareth*, observes Luke's focus on the joy of salvation, seen in moments like the Magnificat (Luke 1:46-55), the angelic proclamation to the shepherds (Luke 2:10-11), and the resurrection appearances: *"In Luke, the joy of the Gospel arises from the certainty that God's mercy is for all, reaching the farthest corners of the world and the human heart."* Pope Francis, in *Evangelii Gaudium*, draws heavily on Luke's portrayal of Jesus as the compassionate Savior to inspire the Church's mission of mercy: *"The Gospel of Luke shows us the God who is close to us, who seeks the lost sheep and rejoices in its return. This is the heart of evangelization."*

The Christology of the Gospel of Luke offers a portrait of Jesus as the compassionate, universal, and Spirit-filled Savior. Patristic, medieval, and modern commentaries reveal how Luke's narrative invites believers to encounter Christ, who bridges the human and divine, offering salvation to all.

As we delve into this Gospel, may we, like Mary, keep all these things in our hearts (Luke 2:19) and, like the disciples on the road to Emmaus, encounter the risen Christ in the breaking of the bread (Luke 24:30-31).

John P. Cush, STD
Saint Joseph's Seminary and College, Yonkers, New York
November 22, 2024

Eight Themes in Luke's Gospel
to Look for while Preaching

- **Jesus as the Universal Savior:**
  Luke's Gospel emphasizes the universality of Jesus' mission, as seen in the genealogy tracing Him to Adam and the inclusion of Gentiles in His ministry (Luke 7:1-10).

- **Jesus and the Kingdom:**
  Luke's Gospel emphasizes the Kingdom of God that Jesus came to bring and that he is in Himself (Luke 1:32-33, 4:20, 7:14-15, 9:34-36, 20:34-38)

- **Jesus as the Compassionate Savior through the Parables:**
  The parables of the Good Samaritan (Luke 10:25-37) and the Prodigal Son (Luke 15:11-32) exemplify Christ's mercy, offering a model for Christian discipleship. Charles Dickens described the parable of the Prodigal Son as follows: "It is the finest short story ever written."

- **The Cost of Discipleship:**
  The disciple who follows the Blessed Lord had to witness (Luke 5:10), demonstrate compassion (Luke 13:19), and show gratitude (Luke 7:44-47).

- **The Holy Spirit and Jesus:**
  From His conception (Luke 1:35) to His public ministry (Luke 4:18-19), Jesus is depicted as Spirit-filled, underscoring His divine mission.

- **Jesus in Prayer:**
  Luke often portrays Jesus in prayer, reflecting His intimate relationship with the Father and modeling radical dependence on God.

- **The Gospel of Mary and the Women:**
  Our Lady is the "co-star" of this Gospel. It is said that Our Lady told the stories in the Gospel to the Evangelist Saint Luke in Ephesus. Note also the importance of all the women whom Our Lord encounters in the Gospel.

- **The Gospel of Poor and the Outcast**:
  Note that the poor shepherds come to the newborn King Luke 2:8). Our Lord Jesus befriends the outcasts (i.e. the sinful woman in Luke 7; the Ten lepers (Luke 17); the blind man (Luke 18)) and Zacchaeus (Luke 19)

First Sunday of Advent

There's a tremendous sense of urgency in the message given to us in our readings on this first Sunday of the liturgical season of Advent. The basic message is the Kingdom of God is at hand. And what is the Kingdom of God? Perhaps we might wish to adjust our interrogatory pronoun from "what" to a more appropriate "who." Who is the Kingdom of God? It is Jesus. He is the messenger and the message; he is the teacher and what is taught; he is the preacher and what is preached. And what does Jesus come to bring- nothing less than himself- he is salvation, and he manifests this salvation in his words and in his deeds.

And this arrival of the Messiah in the midst of Israel requires a radical recognition of the identity of Jesus as the Christ and, if we take seriously who it is that Jesus is and what it is that he stands for, then there must be a radical change in life, a true repentance. The early follower of Christ would have a real sense of the urgency of repentance in order to embrace the Kingdom of God.

As we could expect, the sense of eschatology, of the four last things (death, judgment, Heaven, hell), was so much greater in the early Church. These followers of the Way, who daily were risking their lives because they believed in Christ, who were considered enemies of the state due to their faith, truly believed that, at any moment, Jesus, King of Glory and Lord of the World would descend, just as he had ascended to judge each man according to his deeds.

Naturally enough, when Jesus didn't come back, after a year, after ten years, after fifty years, even as followers of a religion considered a dangerous, seditious cult, followers of the Way began to become complacent. They settled into their daily routines and the concerns of daily life became more and more important. They began to focus in on the little things of life, naturally enough, and began to miss the big picture. The Christians in Corinth, in Rome, in Ephesus, and in other places began to forget that, at any moment, the bridegroom could come again, like a thief in the night, and they could be caught wallowing in the mire of their own sin. Made for immortality, they could stuck in immorality.

As history progresses, this is even more true. When the danger of being Christian seemingly fades, when Christianity becomes, in a sense, mainstream, like after the Emperor Constantine's edict tolerating Christianity, and, indeed throughout most of western civilization, instead of the big picture, we put our focus in on the little things, as important as they might be and miss the forest for the trees.

The same is true today, even with the reality that being a Christian today, in the Middle East, in Africa, and in other places, can and might get you killed. In the U.S. today, in the age of the cult of political correctness, we may not be physically killed for our faith, but we are considered completely irrelevant and the enemy by a large portion of society. We have lost that eschatological edge, and, I think, we need to reclaim it as soon as possible, if we are to regain the proper focus in the Christian life.

The Protestant theologian, Paul Tillich, asked what is our area of ultimate concern. What did he mean by this term, "the area of our ultimate concern"? It's actually quite simple- naturally enough, as we go through life, we, as responsible adults, have many concerns, for instance, our health, our family's safety and wellbeing, our financial security. These are concerns, but if one were to ask a person what his or her ultimate concern really was, it might be harder to articulate. According to Tillich, true religion, defined by him as "the state of being grasped by ultimate concern," is the area of our ultimate concern. The area of ultimate concern is that upon which we base our lives; it should be the guiding factor in all our life decisions; it should be that "pearl of great price," that which will perdure after all the other concerns of our lives, as important, as they are have faded.

So, what's our area of ultimate concern? What's really our ultimate concern? If it's not the salvation of our immortal soul, then we need to reevaluate our lives. John the Baptist stands as one who reminds us of what and who our area of ultimate concern has to be- the Lord Jesus Christ. May we use this Advent season to reclaim our eschatological edge.

Second Sunday of Advent

In the Gospel we proclaim this day with which the Lord has blessed us, we see the true beauty of the work of the Evangelist whose telling of the Good News we have this liturgical year — St. Luke. Look at all the details he gives us in the Gospel today, all meant to situate the reader in the time period.

Saint Luke the Evangelist writes: *"In the fifteenth year of the reign of Tibe'rius Caesar, Pontius Pilate being governor of Judea, and Herod being tetrarch of Galilee, and his brother Philip tetrarch of the region of Iturae'a and Trachoni'tis, and Lysa'nias tetrarch of Abile'ne, in the high-priesthood of Annas and Ca'iaphas, the word of God came to John the son of Zechari;ah in the wilderness; and he went into all the region about the Jordan, preaching a baptism of repentance for the forgiveness of sins."*

The Evangelist gives us all those details not only because Luke loves the stories (our Catholic tradition holds that the Blessed Virgin Mary was the main source of his information and some in the Byzantine tradition believe Saint Luke was the first iconographer, writing [which is what the Eastern Church calls painting] the first picture of Our Lady), but also because of his audience. Written around the year 85 AD (roughly 15 years after Mark's Gospel) during the reign of Emperor Domitian, Luke is writing for "Theophilus," the friend of God, those who want to know more about Christ Jesus, who are primarily during Luke's time a Gentile audience.

As I mentioned, the Evangelist Saint Luke loves history. That's why he mentions each of these people, like Tiberius Caesar, Pontius Pilate, Herod, etc., because each of them is a historical character. No one with a sense of Roman (or even world history) could ever claim that these leaders did not exist. This is important because it helps situate the Lord Jesus into history as well. Say what one will — no one can deny that a historical figure by the name of Jesus of Nazareth existed. Whether or not one wishes to place faith in him as the Incarnation of God, that is a matter of faith. But no one in his or her right mind can ever doubt that Jesus was an actual historical figure.

History matters. (And I say that not only because I teach Church history.) There are two ways to look at history — one way is to see it as a series of unconnected events, random occurrences that really don't have any meaning. The other way, the proper way, in my opinion, is to view history through the lens of Kairos. Yes, everything matters — the fact that you and I are here in this place, right here, right now, worshipping our God in spirit and truth, together, is part of chronology.

The fact we are now living through this odd time in the history of the world, filled with pandemics and other events matters. Why? Because together we are living in the moment of Kairos, our own personal salvation histories, all tied into the larger scheme of Salvation History in which the Lord of Time allows us to occupy. Perhaps in our prayer today, we might wish to acknowledge our history, both our personal ones, the history of the Church, and that of the world. Do we live like the philosopher Leibniz states: "in the best of all possible worlds?" Who knows? Regardless, this is the world we have been given. Thank God for our histories which are tied intrinsically to salvation history.

Third Sunday of Advent

We continue in the Gospel passage taken from the Evangelist Saint Luke right where we left off last week — with Saint John the Baptist, the pontifex (the bridge) between the Old and the New Testament. John, as we know, is the last and greatest of the prophets. He stands in the tradition of the great prophets, like Isaiah, Elijah, Hosea, and Zechariah. In order to understand the role of John the Baptist, we might wish to go back to see what the role of the prophet was in the Old Testament.

You see, in the beginning of the Israelite religion, the Lord God had the patriarchs: Abraham, Isaac, and Jacob (Israel). Later, Joseph brings the smallest of the nations, the People of Israel into Egypt in order to save them. They were men who had experienced the very presence of God and were able to lead his people and found the nation.

Later, we see in the history of Israel the great man, Moses, who leads his people from slavery in Egypt to the Promised Land, a place into which he himself cannot enter. After the death of Moses, the Lord God raises up the Judges, who are basically charismatic warlords, men, and women whom God would raise up from the community of Israel to rule for a specific reason and for a specific period of time.

Then, into the picture, we have the Israelites wanting to become like every other nation, to have a king whom they can see and touch and hear. The Lord God doesn't want to do this. Israel has a king and it is the Lord God. Yahweh, God himself, warns Israel that if they keep asking for a king, all they will get is trouble, and, eventually, due to their hardness of heart, God grants Kings to the People of Israel, and, as we see, each one is worse than the next! Even the best of the kings like David and Solomon aren't really completely faithful and sinless and whoa upon whoa come to the Nation of Israel.

Now, at the same time that God permits a king for the people of Israel, he also raises up prophets. The Greek word *prophetes* means "one who speaks before others," so the prophet was the one who communicated the Word of God. He was not sanctified for this role by the altar, but by possession of and by the Word of God.

To be blunt, the role of the prophet was to be a nudge. To be that annoying presence in the community always calling back Israel to the reality that, above all else, "God is King!," and no one other! They did this by radical deeds and stirring words, and, now that the time of salvation has come and the long-awaited Messiah is in the midst, John the Baptist, this last, this forerunner of the Christ, this friend of the Bridegroom, is no different. The Baptist, with his stirring words and outlandish appearance, brings attention not to himself, but to the Word of God.

John's role is to bring attention to the one who is coming after him, the one who is mightier than he, the Messiah whose sandal strap he is not even worthy to loosen. He is not the Bridegroom. He is the friend of the Bridegroom, the best man who gets everything ready for the coming festivities, which is the coming of the Kingdom of God.

A question then for each and every one of us: do we pay attention to the prophets, those who call us back and remind us that God and

God alone is King, in our lives? Are we open to the example of the holy men and women in our own everyday lives? God is revealing his will each day through so many people in our lives, both within and without the walls of his Church.

Are we willing to listen, to be fascinated by them, just like Herod was, even though he was constantly being chastised by the Friend of the Bridegroom, John the Baptist? Look for the prophets in our midst — they are there if only we have the eyes to see and the ears to hear.

Fourth Sunday of Advent

In the epistle, the second reading of todays' Mass, we hear from the Letter to the Hebrews. It is always amusing to hear lectors at Mass state: "A Reading from the Letter of Saint Paul to the Hebrews," and I must admit that I have at private Masses when I have no readers and I have to proclaim the epistle myself, I also have slipped into this! We are so used to all the epistles being written by Saint Paul the Apostle, but, to be honest, no one really knows who exactly was the Divinely Inspired author behind this text.

Some, like Saint Jerome, hold that it is indeed Saint Paul. Other Patristic writers like Origen call that into doubt, and still others who have studied the text claim the Pope Saint Clement of Rome or Saint Luke the Evangelist or even Priscilla, mentioned by Saint Paul in his Epistle to the Romans might be candidates as the author of the text.

In the long run, it really doesn't matter. We do know that, ultimately, God is the real author, working through the Divinely Inspired anonymous author, using the talents, knowledge, and style of the human author to communicate what God intended and only what God intended. Most likely, this epistle is one of the earliest biblical texts of the New Testament, written around 63-64 AD.

Why was this epistle written? It was written for those believers in the Hebrew scriptures and in Christ Jesus who were beginning to doubt whether or not Jesus Christ could be the Messiah. This was because Jesus was just so different than what the majority of the faithful people of Israel had expected.

The Divinely Inspired author of the Epistle to the Hebrews tries to encourage his listeners by reminding them that the long-awaited

Messiah of Israel was also meant to be not only a king, but a priest, one far greater than the Levitical priests who have to stand at the altar in the Temple and offer sacrifice day after day.

No, the Lord Jesus by his one, single, sacrifice on the altar of his cross, shows himself to be the priest, the victim, and the altar himself. He is priest and he is also the king who is to come; therefore, these Hebrew Christians need to have patience and faith that the Lord's coming is not a delay, even though we might view it as a delay.

With all of this information in mind concerning the author and the purpose of the Epistle to the Hebrews, a question for us today — who is the Jesus whom we await? Is he the just judge who will reward us for our fidelity and punish us for our unrepented inequity? Is he the gentle Good Shepherd who searches in mercy for each of us who are lost sheep, longing to bring us back to his fold? Is he the newborn King, gently laid in a manger, no crib for his bed, under the protective gaze of Saint Joseph the Just Man and his Blessed Virgin Mary, the Help of Christians? Is he the Man of Sorrows whose arms are stretched out on the Cross in an embrace of love for you and me, permitting the red rain that is his Most Precious Blood to wash us clean of our sins?

The answer to all of these questions and more is yes. Jesus Christ is Lord. Jesus Christ is the incarnation, the taking on of flesh of the Second Person of the Most Blessed Trinity. He is God himself coming down to us on a mission to save us. Jesus is the priest, he is the altar, and he is the victim.

He is the Lord God of all and we await him in only a few more days at Christmas.

Immaculate Conception

As a Christian people, there is no single individual whom we give more honor to than the Blessed Virgin Mary. Since the early Church, the clear teaching in our doctrine is that, from the moment of her conception in the womb of Saint Ann, her mother, Mary was freed from the stain of original sin, so that she could be the spotless, sinless vessel to carry the Son of God made flesh, Our Lord Jesus Christ. Mary herself is the Immaculate Conception.

Some people, unfortunately, get the concept of the Immaculate Conception confused with the concept of the Virgin Birth. No, the Virgin Birth of Our Lord Jesus is the logical consequence of the fact that Mary is the Immaculate Conception. Conceived and born without the sin of hubris, of pride, inherited from our first parents, Our Blessed Lady, Mary, never suffered from Original Sin, the state that the rest of us inherited from the fall of our primordial parents, Adam and Eve.

The Catechism of the Catholic Church (490-493) defines clearly defines the Immaculate Conception and tells us in order to be the mother of Jesus, Mary was given special gifts from God. When the angel Gabriel greeted her, he called her "full of grace," showing she was filled with God's favor to accept this unique role.

Over time, the Church has recognized that Mary was free from original sin from the very start of her life. This belief, known as the *Immaculate Conception*, was officially declared by Pope Pius IX in 1854. He proclaimed that Mary, by a special grace from God and through the future merits of Jesus, was preserved from original sin from the moment she was conceived.

Mary's holiness, which began from her conception, comes entirely from her relationship with Christ. God the Father blessed her in a unique way through Jesus, choosing her to be pure and devoted in love even before creation began. In the Eastern Church, Mary is honored as "the All-Holy" (*Panagia*), seen as entirely free from sin and uniquely formed by the Holy Spirit. By God's grace, she lived her entire life without personal sin.

Therefore, when we hear that the conception of Our Lord, Jesus Christ in the womb of Blessed Mary, we recognize that this is not the doctrine of the Immaculate Conception, but that of the Virgin Birth. And, we recall that, from Catholic Sacred Tradition and dogma, we know that Mary, the Mother of Jesus, the Mother of God, is perpetually virgin, before, during, and after childbirth.

As was mentioned in the Catechism definition of the Immaculate Conception listed above, we know that His Holiness, Pope Pius IX in 1854 declared the Immaculate Conception of the Blessed Virgin Mary as an infallible dogma of the Church, one of the only two times in the history of the Catholic Church that this had occurred.

For us as Americans, we should hold the Immaculate Conception as very dear. Our Lady, under the title of the Immaculate Conception, was declared the Patroness of the United States of America. In fact, it is one of the two Holy Days of Obligation that must always be a "Day of Obligation," even if it falls on a Monday or a Saturday. We in the United States of America love Our Lady under the title of the Immaculate Conception. And we know that, despite our failings, she loves us. And so, we pray:

Remember, O most gracious Virgin Mary,
that never was it known
that anyone who fled to thy protection,
implored thy help,
or sought thy intercession,
was left unaided.
Inspired by this confidence
I fly unto thee,
O Virgin of virgins, my Mother.
To thee do I come,
before thee I stand,
sinful and sorrowful.
O Mother of the Word Incarnate,
despise not my petitions,
but in thy mercy hear and answer me.
Amen.

Our Lady of Guadalupe

As we celebrate the Feast of Our Lady of Guadalupe, we honor Mary, who appeared to a humble indigenous man, Juan Diego, on the hills of Tepeyac in 1531. In this appearance, Mary chose to come not in grand robes or rich garments, but as a humble, mestiza woman, a mother who spoke the language of her people. In doing so, she showed us that God comes to us where we are, meeting us in our own culture, language, and life circumstances.

When Our Lady appeared to Juan Diego, she brought not only words of comfort but also a message of hope, unity, and love that transcended divisions of race, status, and wealth. She appeared to the indigenous people of Mexico, who were marginalized, oppressed, and often overlooked. Her appearance affirmed their dignity and worth, reminding them that they were not forgotten by God. Through Mary, God reached out with a tender embrace to the poor and the overlooked, assuring them that they are deeply loved and valued.

Our Lady's message is profoundly relevant to us today. She reminds us that, as disciples of Christ, we are called to see and serve those who are often unseen and unheard. Her call to Juan Diego to build a church at Tepeyac was a call to create a space where everyone could experience the presence and love of God. And in this church, all people would find welcome and peace—a reminder that our communities today should be places of refuge, compassion, and mercy for all who seek God.

Our Lady of Guadalupe also shows us the power of faith and perseverance. Despite Juan Diego's hesitation and the challenges he faced, he trusted in Mary's message and followed her guidance. Even when others doubted him, he remained faithful, and through his courage, a great miracle unfolded. The roses that he carried in his tilma, in the dead of winter, bloomed as signs of Mary's presence and her promise. When we face challenges and doubts, may we find strength in her example and remember that God can bring new life and miracles even in our darkest winters.

Today, we celebrate Mary as the patroness of the Americas, our mother and protector, who is always with us, ready to intercede on our behalf. Just as she embraced Juan Diego with motherly love, so too does she embrace each one of us, with all our struggles, fears, and hopes. Her presence calls us to be people of hope and reconciliation, to break down walls of division, and to create communities that reflect the love of Christ.

As we reflect on Our Lady's appearance at Tepeyac, let us renew our own commitment to walk in her footsteps—reaching out to the poor, uplifting the marginalized, and living lives rooted in love, compassion, and humility. May we, like Juan Diego, be humble messengers of God's love in the world, bringing the light of Christ to those around us.

Our Lady of Guadalupe, pray for us, that we may follow in your example and bring Christ's love to a world in need.

Christmas

This evening, we celebrate the Nativity of the Lord in the flesh. As we believe, from all eternity, God exists. God exists as one God in three persons, Father, Son, and Holy Spirit, from all eternity. The Father, the lover, the begetter, loves and knows the Son, the beloved, the only-begotten, from all eternity. The bond of love and knowledge that exists from all eternity between the Father and Son is the Holy Spirit. This is the Triune God in whom we believe.

Out of love, God deigns to create the world and all reality. By the will of the Father and the work of the Holy Spirit, all things visible and invisible come into being. God, who is all good, creates for one reason, his very nature, love. All that God creates by his Word, his Son, is good. God himself pronounces it good.

The highest of all of God's creation was the human being, male and female, created in God's image. At first, the man and the woman lived in that original justice, that peace with God, but through the work of the fallen angel, Lucifer, and through their own fear and pride, man and woman, original sin enters the world. And so begins the long slog through salvation history.

Patriarchs, judges, kings, and prophets, exiles, and sufferings all lead to that day, when at the appointed time, the Father sends the Son, born of a woman, a virgin, into the world, at the Annunciation, which we heard proclaimed at the Mass of Fourth Sunday of Advent. In the Immaculate womb of the Blessed Virgin, time and eternity meet, truth and peace kiss, and the long reign of sin and death is conquered. The New Eve, Mary, gives us the New Adam, who is

Christ. Our weak frail human nature, at the Nativity of the Lord, is caught up into the eternal Godhead.

This baby, this newborn King whom we hail in the manger, he is a danger. He is a danger. This child is dangerous because nothing is as lovable as a baby. Babies, by their nature, are cute and cuddly. It's as if they have a little something about them that makes people want to take care of them. If children were lovable, even more so must have been the most adorable Jesus. This little Lord Jesus, asleep in the hay, is dangerous. Why? Because if we take seriously what goes on in the Nativity, then our whole little world will have to change; the world as we know it will have to change' Think about it: in our fallen human condition, how do we know the world, in its fallen human state, in our fallen human nature: we know it as violent, filled with hatred, with anger and avarice, with lust, shame; a world of sin. This Earth is groaning under the weight of it all.

Into the darkness comes this very little word, this *logos*, the light of the world. We have the God of paradox present in our midst. God, all powerful, becomes all weak as a baby; God, all wise, becomes all needy, as a baby; God, who is eternal, enters into time as a baby. And he does this, all the while remaining God.

The incarnate God: God becomes one like us in all things but sin. "Nothing human is foreign to him." He knows our pain, our fear, our suffering. He who did not know sin becomes sin itself. The same Christ who is born in the wood of the manger, poor and naked, wrapped in cloths, is the same Christ who died on the wood of the Cross, poor and naked, bloodied, "cursed, defiled, bruised, defiled," as the *Stabat Mater* reminds us. This child, born to us, unto us a Son is given, is a promise and a pledge, but also a challenge. This Christmas, bathed in Love's pure light, may we accept this challenge.

Sunday in the Octave of Christmas

A priest who is a friend of mine was the celebrant of Mass on Christmas Day in his parish and proclaimed the Gospel with which we are presented this Sunday, the Solemnity of the Lord's Nativity. There are several Masses of Christmas, each with its own set of readings. The Mass for Christmas Day is titled "Mass During the Day," and has the Prologue of the Gospel of John as its Gospel.

A parishioner was angered, enraged that the deacon at Mass read this prologue, rather than what he had come to hear, what he had expected to hear, namely the Gospel account of Christ's birth, taken from the Gospel of Luke. The pastor explained that there are several readings that could be done for the Masses of Christmas and that, if he stopped to think about it, isn't this particular pericope from the Gospel of John, with its prologue speaking of the eternal Word becoming incarnate, really what Christmas is all about, anyway? The parishioner did not agree and sadly left, aggrieved.

No, although we might wish to hear the story of the long-awaited Messiah's humble birth in Bethlehem, with its angels and shepherds, and we might wish to see the Nativity pageant played out in our midst by youngsters, it is good that, in her wisdom, Mother Church offers us the prologue of John's Gospel for our reflection on Christmas Day.

In the Extraordinary Form of the Mass, this Gospel is read, not just at Christmas Mass, but indeed at the conclusion of every Mass. Why? I believe it was for one reason: to remind us, who have just received the Body of Christ, to become in our words and in our deeds He whom we have just received.

We are called to make incarnate, to make flesh, the Eternal Word who was from the beginning, allowing Him to live in us, just as He did in the spotless, immaculate womb of the Blessed Virgin Mary.

The philosopher, Msgr. Robert Sokolowski, in his book *Christian Faith and Human Understanding: Studies on the Eucharist, Trinity, and the Human Person* (2006), suggests that we use the words of this preface when we make a prayer of thanksgiving after Mass, not just together as a common liturgical experience when the Extraordinary Form of the Mass is offered, but also at every Mass in the Ordinary Form that is celebrated in every parish and chapel daily.

This private thanksgiving prayer of the Catholic, reflecting deeply on the mystery of Christ, who is living inside him or her after the reception of Holy Communion is an essential aspect of the Mass and is sadly, often forgotten in parishes today.

What do I mean by an act of thanksgiving after Communion? How can the Prologue of John's Gospel help?

Use the time of silence, which is an essential part of the Mass, the time between the ending of Communion Antiphon (or Communion Hymn) and the praying of the Collect After Communion by the priest who is celebrating the Mass, to kneel down, if we can, or sit quietly in the realization of what exactly has just occurred to us at that moment of the Mass. This can also be done, and beautifully so, when we take some time after Mass is concluded to remain in the church or chapel and prayerfully reflect.

At that moment, with the Lord living in us, we are as close to Heaven as we are ever going to be on this earthly plane of existence. The ultimate gift, the one we should receive not only at Christmas, but also on every Sunday and Solemnity, has been given to us. The

Word, who was from the beginning, the One through whom all things were made, the One who is Life, Jesus, is living inside of us.

Father Jean-Jacques Olier, S.S., founder of the Sulpicians, a group of priests who are missioned to seminary work, expresses this sentiment beautifully. He writes: "O Jesus, living in Mary, come and live in your servants, in the spirit of holiness, in the fullness of your power, in the perfection of your ways, in the truth of your virtues, in the communion of your mysteries. Rule over every adverse power, in your Spirit, for the glory of the Father. Amen."

Praying the words of the Prologue powerfully reminds us of the reality of what is occurring spiritually – and indeed, even physically – to us. Praying the words can also, in the midst of our troubled world, give us hope. "And this life was the light of the human race; the light shines in the darkness, and the darkness has not overcome it" (John 1: 4-5).

There are problems, there are difficulties, there are fears and anxieties, but the Lord is right there with us, our food for the journey.

Praying the words of the Prologue can remind us that, just as the Eternal, Incarnate Word came to His own, and was rejected, so too, even by our own families and friends, we will be rejected when we try to become He whom we receive. Yet, we have confident assurance that the Lord is right there in our midst.

"But to those who did accept him, he gave power to become children of God, to those who believe in his name, who were born not by natural generation nor by human choice nor by a man's decision, but of God" (John 1: 12-13).

This Prologue of John's Gospel may not be what we expect to hear at Mass on Christmas Day, but it is perhaps exactly what we need to hear, reminding us that, in the Eucharist we receive, we become living tabernacles of the Most High God. We gain the ability – through reception of Holy Communion – to see Christ in and to be Christ to one another.

What better gift could we get for Christmas!

Feast of the Holy Family

The Gospel passage presented to us today is taken from the second chapter of the Gospel according to Saint Luke. Recall that, in our Catholic tradition, it is thought that the main source of the information on the life of Christ Jesus in Luke's Gospel comes from the Blessed Virgin Mary, the Mother of Christ Jesus. Perhaps this is why the narrative which is presented to us for our reflection is so detailed and so personal. It is, in many ways, only a story that a parent, a mother or a father, could tell later on about their child.

In this passage, we read that, having gone to Jerusalem with his parents for the feast of the Passover, the twelve year old Jesus disappears from their watch. Recall also that the last time in the Gospel we had heard about Jesus, he was only a newborn child and that the next time we hear about him, he is already a man about thirty years old, about to begin his public ministry.

Yes, the boy Jesus departs from the side of his parents, almost in a way prefiguring the manner in which he would leave home in Nazareth to announce his Gospel of the coming Kingdom of God. Where do his worried parents eventually find the young Messiah? Where else but "his Father's house," the Temple of Jerusalem, the place which the nation of Israel believed to be the holiest of holy places, the place that in times past contained the Ark of the Covenant, lost now in Israelite antiquity, its final disposition lost to one of the land's many conquerors.

However, the Temple is filled again today with the glory of the Lord, with something, no- someone far greater than the Ark of the Covenant. In the physical structure which held the Holy of Holies stands the Holy One of God, God himself made flesh for us and for our salvation. And what is the young Messiah doing in the Temple area when Joseph and the Blessed Virgin discover him? He who is the wisdom from on high is teaching the teachers, exposing them to true teaching by his presence.

Jesus, we are told, "increased in wisdom and in stature, and in favor with God and man." We should stop and wonder about what do we as the Catholic Church believe about the knowledge of Jesus. The sure and certain guide that is *The Catechism of the Catholic Church* (472-474) clearly explains:

This human soul that the Son of God assumed is endowed with a true human knowledge. As such, this knowledge could not in itself be unlimited: it was exercised in the historical conditions of his existence in space and time. This is why the Son of God could, when he became man, "increase in wisdom and in stature, and in favor with God and man", and would even have to inquire for himself about what one in the human condition can learn only from experience. This corresponded to the reality of his voluntary emptying of himself, taking "the form of a slave".

But at the same time, this truly human knowledge of God's Son expressed the divine life of his person. "The human nature of God's Son, not by itself but by its union with the Word, knew and showed forth in itself everything that pertains to God."

By its union to the divine wisdom in the person of the Word incarnate, Christ enjoyed in his human knowledge the fullness of understanding of the eternal plans he had come to reveal. What he admitted to not knowing in this area, he elsewhere declared himself not sent to reveal.

Being the Messiah did not come as a surprise to Jesus! No, Jesus is Lord, he is God made flesh, and he is the savior of the world. Today's Gospel demonstrates that the Holy One of God when he visits the Temple and instructs the teachers of the Law replaces the Holy of Holies. Jesus is fully human and fully divine. He is one divine Person with two natures, human and divine, a man like us in all things but sin. Never lose sight of the Saving Divinity of the Son of God, the Word made Flesh, the Splendor of the Father.

Solemnity of Mary, Mother of God

This passage, "And Mary kept all these things, reflecting on them in her heart" (Luke 2:19), speaks to Mary's deep interior life—a constant dialogue with God in which she ponders the mysteries of Christ's life. Through the lens of Pope John Paul II, Pope Paul VI, and Pope Francis, we can explore how Mary's interior reflection models the essence of faith and love.

Pope Paul VI, in *Marialis Cultus*, emphasized Mary's role as a model of contemplation for every believer. He described how Mary's heart was open to God's mystery, and in her meditation, she pondered the unfathomable depths of Christ's mission. He said: "She is the model of that interior life which is the prerequisite for hearing the voice of God in the depth of one's heart and for following His call." Paul VI invites us to imitate Mary's "contemplative silence," reminding us that in a world full of distractions, true understanding of God's plan unfolds in quiet reflection.

Like Mary, we are called to keep the events of our lives in a place of quiet prayer, allowing God to unfold His wisdom within us. Mary teaches us that the journey of faith requires a listening heart, receptive to God's ways, especially when they surpass our understanding.

Pope John Paul II, in *Redemptoris Mater*, explored Mary's unique experience of faith, one of constant contemplation of her Son's mystery. He spoke of Mary as a "pilgrim of faith," whose entire life was a continuous 'yes' to God. John Paul II noted, "In her heart, Mary awaited with deep love the fulfillment of that mystery which had been revealed to her" (*Redemptoris Mater*, 17). For him, Mary's heart embodies an openness to God's love, mystery, and will—a reflection that turns into a complete gift of self.

Mary's contemplation teaches us that faith is not merely intellectual but involves the whole heart and soul. In times of mystery, suffering, or uncertainty, we, like Mary, are called to say "yes" in faith, trusting that God's love will guide and sustain us, even when His ways are beyond our sight.

Pope Francis often speaks of Mary as a model of mercy and tenderness, particularly in her heart's attitude toward Jesus and the Church. In *Evangelii Gaudium*, he reflects on how Mary's heart understands the sorrows and joys of the faithful, her compassion born from deeply pondering her Son's life and passion. Pope Francis sees Mary's heart as an "open heart, wounded by her Son's suffering, which makes her tender and attentive to each of us."

From Pope Francis's perspective, Mary's pondering heart encourages us to open ourselves in mercy to others. Like Mary, who kept all things in her heart, we can carry the joys and sufferings of others in prayer, becoming compassionate reflections of God's love in the world.

Through the reflections of Popes Paul VI, John Paul II, and Francis, we see that Mary's contemplation is not passive but an active engagement with God's presence. Her heart is a model for our faith journey, teaching us to hold all things—our questions, joys, and trials—in our hearts, trusting that God's mystery will be revealed in time. Mary's silent, patient love calls each of us to a deeper intimacy with God, guiding us to live our faith with an open, trusting, and compassionate heart.

Epiphany

I'm here today to speak about one of the most heinous offences that occur during the Christmas season. Year after year, it goes on, and, sadly, very few people have the courage to stand up and say no to it. I'm not speaking about the commercialization of Christmas, with sales and decorations beginning right after Halloween; I'm not referring to the generic greetings of "Happy Holidays," which, in our politically correct society has become the norm, even, at times for Christians to one another. No, I'm referring to something, sadly, I have to admit, that even I have done. Perhaps even you yourselves are guilty of this particular offense as well.

To what horrible action might I be referring you might be asking yourself? The answer is simple: re-gifting. It goes on and on and no one will put a stop to it! It starts out rather simply, of course. I'll give an example in the life of a priest, especially a priest who teaches- "let's get Father a black gloves or handkerchiefs." Well, after a while, Father winds up with ten pairs of gloves or twenty handkerchiefs, so he begins to give them away as gifts, recycling the original gift, passing it off as a thoughtful present which he himself has bought, carefully plotting and praying that he doesn't give the gift back to the one who has originally given it to him in the first place! Yes, it's true. Re-gifting goes on and on and on in an endless cycle. For instance, it's been proven that there are only five Christmas fruitcakes in existence- they all just keep getting re-gifting from family to family.

Today, however, we celebrate a special feast in this Christmas season- the Epiphany of the Lord. And on this feast, we are not only permitted to re-gift, it is expected! What do I mean by this? It's very simple: at Christmas, we were given a great gift- the gift of Jesus Christ Himself. Our God, omniscient, omnipotent, deigns to share in our mortal nature through the miracle of the Incarnation. God becomes one like us in all things, while still remaining God. Listen to the words of the preface of this Mass: "(w)hen he appeared in our mortal nature, you made us new by the glory of his immortal nature." It is through the gift of the Word becoming flesh, a gift far more valuable than gold, frankincense and myrrh, that we are saved. The Lord has been revealed to us as the light to the nations. We are called to follow that star of salvation that He Himself is.

Like these wise men, these three kings, these magi about whom we read, we are called not to keep this star to ourselves. In following that star, in the reception of the gift that Christ is in Himself, we are called to take that gift of Christ that we receive and to re-gift it, to share it with everyone whom we meet. How do we do that? Simply by becoming light itself, by permitting the "New Light that was coming into this world" to transfigure us into new sons and daughters of his. How will we re-gift the ultimate gift? Each of us has to answer that for him or herself each day in all of the situations in which we find ourselves.

The best explanation of this feast was given to me years ago when I was a small child. Christmas is like when a baby is born and the new mom and dad just want to hold and touch and marvel in the new little wonder that the Lord has helped them bring into the world. Epiphany is when that mom and dad take that baby and share him or her with the grandparents, relatives and friends, saying "Look at this gift that we've been given." Today, let's give we give that gift of that newborn King to all whom we meet. Re-gift that gift- after all, it's the one time it's perfectly acceptable.

Baptism of the Lord

Today, we conclude the Christmas season with the feast of the Baptism of the Lord. So, if your Christmas decorations are still up, you can start thinking about taking them down. In the old liturgical calendar, February 2, the feast of the Presentation of the Lord was considered by most to be the absolutely last day of the Christmas season. So, if your tree is still up in April, don't say you weren't warned.

This feast of the Baptism of the Lord in the United States used to coincide with the National Vocation Awareness Week. This week, to my knowledge, has been moved to the Easter season. However, many of the themes which I think come out of this feast can help each of us, no matter what our state in life, come to discover our own unique vocation in the Christian life.

Instead of beginning our focus on the event which is detailed in the Gospel today, namely the inauguration of the Lord Jesus' ministry and the definitive declaration of his union with the Blessed Trinity by God the Father, I'd like us to examine the other main figure in today's Gospel, John the Baptist.

Although only Luke's Gospel actually comes out and states that John was the blood relative, the cousin of the Lord Jesus, we know for certain that there was a strong, intrinsic bond between John the Baptist and Jesus. Jesus Himself proclaims the fact that there is no man born of woman greater than John the Baptist. In fact, there were many, many people who truly believed that John was the Christ and there were many, many people who left everything to go and follow him. One of the reasons why the story of the baptism of the Lord by

John in the Jordan is featured in all four of the Gospels is to serve as a reminder to all that it is Jesus, not John, who is the Holy One of God, the Messiah. John, in all four accounts from the Gospel, is the first to recognize the adult Jesus as Lord, and, in fact, protests vehemently the mere suggestion that he should baptize Jesus.

There must have been a reason why so many people believed that John was the Messiah at first. For starters, he fit the part of the Old Testament prophet much more than did Jesus. John, with his clothes of camel hair and the leather belt around his waist, looked the part. With his diet of wild honey and locust, and, above all, his consistent message of repentance in preparation for the coming of the Kingdom of God, John, perhaps even more so than Jesus, looked like a new version of Hosea, with his outrageous stunts to make his point, or a new Ezekiel, a new Isaiah or, perhaps even more, a new Elijah.

Imagine being John the Baptist. Imagine the whole world hanging on your every word, your every action. Imagine the feeling of power, the feeling of euphoria. They all want you; they all need you. Now, remember that messiahs, or rather people claiming to be the messiah, were a dime a dozen in Jerusalem. Every single Jewish mother was hoping and praying that it would be her little boy who would grow up to be the savior of his people. And, I'd venture to guess, perhaps Elizabeth was the same.

And yet, John does not let the fame, the adulation go to his head. He knows who he is and what it is that he is meant to be. "Not me, but thee, O Lord." "He must increase, I must decrease." Or, as he states in another Gospel passage, "One mightier than I is coming after me. I am not worthy to stoop and loosen the thongs of his sandals. I have baptized you with water; he will baptize you with the Holy Spirit."

John is able to do this because he knows who he is: he is not the messiah, but the forerunner of the Messiah, the last and greatest of the Prophets, the one selected from all eternity to point the way to the Lamb of God, who is going to take away the sins of the world. John knows that he is a beloved child of God Most High, one created in the image and likeness of Almighty God, and one who will be bathed in the most precious blood of the Lamb who will be slain for us men and our salvation. And that's enough for him. This is true humility, true openness to the will of the Lord in our life. This can only come from self-knowledge and confidence in the place that the Lord has for us in the building up of his Kingdom.

How about for us? Do we know, really know, who we are? Do we recognize that we are not the Messiah? That God is God and that we're not God, and thank God for that? Do we recognize that we are creature, not creator, completely totally dependent on the one who loves us, that every breath we take is totally dependent on the gracious will of our Heavenly Father?

The Ancient Greek aphorism "know thyself", is one of the Delphic maxims and was inscribed in the pronaos of the Temple of Apollo at Delphi according to the Greek periegetic writer Pausanias. Do you and I know ourselves, really know ourselves? Do I trust that, for some reason known only to God, in spite of my sinful ways and my human limitations, I was chosen to be his priest, and so too are all my brother priests? Do you in consecrated life recognize that, for no other reason besides the will of the Heavenly Father, you were chosen to be a Bride of Christ, with your vows of poverty, chastity, and obedience, all true eschatological signs of the Kingdom of God which John was born to preach and which Jesus is in his very Divine Person? Do you in your own particular vocation in this Christian life, married, single, recognize who you are, how beautiful you are, another beloved daughter or son of God the Most High?

The 20th century spiritual writer Thomas Merton, after many years of living the Trappist lifestyle, was permitted to leave his abbey to go shopping for his community one day. This is from his work, *Conjectures of a Guilty Bystander*:

> *"In Louisville, at the corner of Fourth and Walnut, in the center of the shopping district, I was suddenly overwhelmed with the realization that I loved all those people, that they were mine and I theirs, that we could not be alien to one another even though we were total strangers. It was like waking from a dream of separateness, of spurious self-isolation in a special world, the world of renunciation and supposed holiness... This sense of liberation from an illusory difference was such a relief and such a joy to me that I almost laughed out loud... I have the immense joy of being man, a member of a race in which God Himself became incarnate. As if the sorrows and stupidities of the human condition could overwhelm me, now I realize what we all are. And if only everybody could realize this! But it cannot be explained. There is no way of telling people that they are all walking around shining like the sun."*

You're all walking around, shining like the sun. Despite sorrow, despite sin, you and I are created in God's image and through baptism are conformed to his likeness. On your worst day, when everything seems to be going wrong, don't lose sight of that.

The Feast of the Presentation of the Lord

Today, as we gather to celebrate the Feast of the Presentation of the Lord, our hearts turn to the profound mystery of Christ's light entering the world. The liturgy invites us to reflect on the fulfillment of God's promises, the joy of salvation, and the transformative power of divine light.

Our readings—Malachi's prophecy, the psalm of glory, the Letter to the Hebrews, and the Gospel of Luke—lead us deeper into this mystery. Let us journey together through these texts, allowing them to illumine our hearts and renew our hope.

Malachi's prophecy proclaims the coming of the Lord to His temple: "He is like a refiner's fire and like fuller's lye." The imagery of purification reminds us that God's light does not merely comfort but also transforms. *The Catechism of the Catholic Church* (695) teaches that the Holy Spirit—symbolized by fire—manifests Christ as the purifying presence in our lives.

Saint Thomas Aquinas, in his *Summa Theologiae* (III, Q. 37), reflects on the Presentation as Christ's submission to the Law, an act of humility that anticipates His ultimate sacrifice. This humility reveals the light of divine love: a love that purifies, renews, and sanctifies.

"Lift up your heads, O gates! Be lifted up, O ancient doors, that the King of glory may come in." These words resound with triumph and anticipation, heralding the arrival of the Messiah.

In this psalm, we find an echo of Pope Francis' call to be "gates" that open to Christ. In *Evangelii Gaudium* (n. 3), he exhorts us to let Christ's light shine in and through us, making the Church a beacon of hope for the world. Like Simeon and Anna, who recognized the light of Christ in the temple, we too are called to welcome Him with open hearts and to share His light with others.

The Letter to the Hebrews reveals Christ's mission to "destroy the one who has the power of death, that is, the devil." By taking on our humanity, Jesus brings the light of salvation into the darkest places of our lives. The CCC (457) reminds us that the Incarnation occurred so that Jesus could save us by reconciling us to God.

Consider the imagery of light in film and poetry. In the film *The Mission* (1986), a scene of reconciliation occurs as a penitent ascends a waterfall, symbolizing the journey from darkness into light. Similarly, John Donne's poem *A Hymn to God the Father* reflects a yearning for divine forgiveness and light: "When Thou hast done, Thou hast not done, for I have more." These artistic expressions resonate with Christ's role as the light who redeems us.

In the Gospel, we encounter Simeon and Anna, two figures who recognize Jesus as the light for revelation to the Gentiles and the glory of Israel. Simeon's canticle, the *Nunc Dimittis,* is a hymn of fulfillment and peace. Christ as the "light of the nations" fulfills the prophecy of Isaiah 49:6, as noted in CCC 529. The Presentation underscores our mission as bearers of this light. Pope Francis, in *Lumen Fidei* (n. 37), emphasizes that faith in Christ illuminates every aspect of human existence, casting out fear and despair.

The Feast of the Presentation calls us to embrace Christ's light and share it with a world yearning for hope. As Thomas Merton wrote in *Thoughts in Solitude,* "My Lord God, I have no idea where I am going... but I believe that the desire to please You does in fact please You." Merton's words remind us that our openness to God's light—even in uncertainty—allows His radiance to shine through us.

Today, let us follow the example of Simeon and Anna, who recognized the light of Christ and proclaimed it with joy. May the light of Christ, the King of glory, purify our hearts, guide our steps, and empower us to bring His love to others. In this Eucharist, we encounter the very light of Christ in the Blessed Sacrament, as the CCC (1374) affirms the Real Presence. May we leave this celebration as vessels of His light, proclaiming with our lives: "The Lord of glory has come; let us rejoice and be glad!"

First Sunday of Lent

The gospel reading presented to us for the First Sunday of Lent is rather familiar to all of us — Our Lord's temptation in the desert. In fact, in every cycle of the lectionary (recall that the "A" cycle offers us Matthew's Gospel, the "B" cycle offers us that of Mark, and in the "C" cycle, which we are in this liturgical year, we are reading from the Gospel of Luke), this important event in the life of Jesus the Christ is proclaimed.

Let's put things into context here for a moment in Luke's Gospel — what's happening in Jesus' life as he experiences the temptation from Satan, the accuser, in the desert: He has just been baptized by John in the Jordan, wherein definitively the voice of the Father is heard, proclaiming for all to hear that "Thou art my beloved Son; with thee I am well pleased."

The Evangelist Luke informs his readers that Jesus is 30 years old; and now, in this fourth chapter of Luke's Gospel, we read that Jesus, before beginning his public ministry, goes into the desert, which, as we know from the Old Testament is a place of danger and uncertainty (look to the experience of the Israelites in Exodus), and stays there for 40 days and 40 nights (recall that the number 40 is significant for the Old Testament, signifying a long period of time). It might also be important to recall that in Luke's Gospel, the story of the temptation of the Lord in the desert is recounted right after the genealogy of Jesus is explored.

The Evangelist Saint Luke, unlike in Matthew's Gospel (which starts with the family line with Abraham in Matthew 1), begins the genealogy with Adam, the first human being. Why would he do this?

Simply to show that Jesus, "the Son of Adam," and only he alone can conquer the universal earthly desire which all humanity suffers — the desire for earthly pleasures and bodily needs and the desire for power and glory. These two desires are the cause of most of the conflicts and wars in human history.

The temptations that the Lord faces in the desert are not temptations to sin. The Lord Jesus is the All-Holy One of God. He is All-Truth, All-Goodness, All-Beauty. Since he is one Divine Person in two natures (human and divine), he is one like us in all things but sin (*The Catechism of the Catholic Church* (467).

The impeccability of the Lord Jesus does not make him more than human; it does not make him less than human. No, in fact, it demonstrates the manner in which the human being was created by God in the Garden of Eden (recall Genesis 1 and 2). Christ has no concupiscence, no inordinate desire to sin, as we fallen human beings do. Therefore, these temptations are not temptations to sin.

So what are these temptations that Our Good Lord faced? First, the temptation to turn stone to bread. Second, the temptation to take charge of all the kingdoms of the world. Third, and finally, to go to the parapet of the Temple and to hurl himself off, and, as the Deceiver so subtly stated, "if you are the Son of God," then the Holy Angels would catch him.

The first temptation is to turn stone to bread. By turning stones to bread, the Lord Jesus would be using his own messianic power to take care of his own physical needs. The second of the temptations is, having seen the powers of this world, to claim the Kingdom, which he is in himself, right here, right now. This is a temptation to earthly power. Jesus is not a political messiah.

The third and final temptation is to test the will of God the Father by performing an act demonstrating Christ's divinity before he has even begun his public ministry.

Lent offers us the opportunity to reflect on the natures and Person of the Christ and how and what kind of Messiah Jesus is for us. Know that he is the Spotless Lamb of God who takes away the sins of the world, who knows our human condition in all things but sin, and is able to help us conquer our own sins and temptations.

Second Sunday of Lent

As in all things, when we read a passage presented to us in the lectionary from the Holy Gospel, we need to place it into the proper context. If we read this particular passage from the Gospel according to the Evangelist Saint Luke, we might get a bit confused. Why would the Lord Jesus take his three closest associates, the Apostles Peter, James, and John, up the mountain to pray and, while they are there, to witness the confirmation of the Lord's identity in the event of his Transfiguration?

We need to look first into the early part of this ninth chapter of Luke's Gospel wherein we read of the Lord's first prediction of his passion in the 22nd verse of this chapter. Before this, life might have seemed like an adventure for Apostles. Filled with fire, they met this man who seemed to know everything about them.

This man from Nazareth, this Jesus, was a prophet, indeed more than a prophet. Simon Peter, the unofficial leader of their apostolic band, when asked by Jesus who the crowds say that he is, does what he usually does — he "one-ups" them all. Peter, to use the nickname that Jesus calls him, goes far beyond what the rest of the disciples are stating. They all say that he is Elijah or John the Baptist or another ancient prophet. Peter goes full-bore and proclaims him the Christ, the anointed one, the Messiah of God.

Then Jesus goes and takes the excitement level down. In verse 22 of this ninth chapter of Luke, he throws these words, which no doubt stung the disciples to the quick: "The Son of Man must suffer greatly and be rejected by the elders, the chief priests, and the scribes, and be killed and on the third day be raised." What is our new leader,

Jesus, who is going to lead all of us into a new Jerusalem and out of Roman control, speaking about?

And Jesus just doesn't stop there with the prediction of his own suffering and death. To be honest, what Jesus was saying there wasn't all that surprising in the reality of his day. Men going around Jerusalem claiming to be the Messiah of God were a dime a dozen in Jesus' day. If they kept challenging the Jewish religious authorities, and, most especially if they were zealots whose religious beliefs led to political insurrectionism, no doubt these "messiahs" would be killed. But what Jesus is saying in verses 23-27, is that not only will he suffer, but so too will all who follow him. And they won't just be rejected, but will suffer the ultimate form of torture — the agony of the cross.

Can you imagine how many of the disciples of the Lord Jesus shook with fear upon hearing those predictions of suffering? How many of them wanted to leave the side of the Lord and to go back to their regular life?

Therefore, when the Lord Jesus takes his "main men," Peter, James, and the beloved disciple, John, up the mountain, it is a kind of divine "pep-talk." These apostles, the most influential perhaps of all the disciples, witness who Jesus truly is. He is the Lord; he is the Son of God, the Word Incarnate, one Divine Person in two natures, human and divine, God himself.

The Apostles, perhaps filled with fear, with doubts, perhaps wondering who they are following to his death and to their own deaths, witness Christ transfigured, filled with the glory of God, shining forth brighter than even Moses did when he met with the Lord. And, to further secure the identity of Jesus in the minds of the

Apostles Peter, James, and John, the Lord meets the two greatest of the figures in the history of Israel, Moses and Elijah.

Christ knows that if we are to be his disciples we must carry our crosses. However, we need not fear that the burden of the cross will overwhelm us and cause us to fall; no, our Lord, our God, our Savior, he who has become our brother, Jesus the Christ, is right next to us, helping us to bear that cross. And this event of the Lord's transfiguration reassures both the Apostles and all of us as Christians.

Third Sunday of Lent

"Sir, leave it for this year also, and I shall cultivate the ground around it and fertilize it; it may bear fruit in the future. If not, you can cut it down."

The Gospel this Sunday strikes a chord that resonates deeply with the season of Lent: *Repent and believe in the Gospel.* Our Lord uses the parable of the barren fig tree to shock us into reflection, much like Flannery O'Connor's "large and startling figures" sought to awaken her readers to divine truths.

The fig tree stands as a stark metaphor for our spiritual lives, urging us to consider whether we are bearing fruit for the Kingdom of God or wasting the soil in which we are planted.

As Flannery O'Connor observed, we live in a world dulled to the distortions of sin. Our modern culture often normalizes what is spiritually harmful, making repentance seem unnecessary or outdated. In such a context, Jesus' parable comes as a jarring wake-up call. His warning about the barren fig tree is not meant to instill fear alone but to compel action. Like O'Connor's shocking narratives, the Gospel's urgency calls us to reevaluate our priorities and seek a radical transformation of heart.

Saint Thomas Aquinas reminds us that God's mercy and justice are not opposed but work in harmony. He writes in the *Summa Theologiae*: *"Justice and mercy are so united that justice without mercy is cruelty, and mercy without justice is the mother of dissolution."* (ST I, Q.21, Art.3) For Aquinas, mercy is more than a passive feeling; it is a divine attribute that demands action. He defines mercy as *"a heartfelt sorrow for another's misfortune, compelling us to act to alle-viate it."* (ST II-II, Q.30, A.1)

When we repent, we open ourselves to God's mercy, but we are also called to imitate that mercy in our lives. Just as God cultivates the soil of our hearts, we are called to tend to others, offering for-giveness, compassion, and love.

In the parable, the gardener's plea for more time reveals God's infinite mercy—a willingness to wait patiently for us to respond to His grace. Yet the warning about cutting down the tree underscores His justice. God desires our salvation, but He respects our free will. The time we have to repent is not infinite; it is a precious gift, meant to lead us to conversion.

Aquinas also emphasizes that true repentance is more than avoiding sin. It involves turning toward God, cultivating virtue, and bearing fruit through love and good works. He teaches that our ul-timate goal is not merely to escape punishment but to grow in holi-ness and union with God, who is our final end.

The Gospel's call to repentance is not a one-time event but an ongoing journey. *The Catechism of the Catholic Church* teaches that this process is part of the work of sanctification: *"The movement of return to God, called conversion and repentance, entails sorrow for and abhorrence of sins committed, and the firm purpose of sinning no more in the future."* (1490). Our lives, like the fig tree, must be culti-vated by God's Word and the sacraments so that we can grow in grace and bear fruit for the Kingdom.

Pope Francis, reflecting on this parable, speaks often about God as the merciful gardener who tends to us with patience: *"The Lord gives each of us the possibility to bear fruit. He patiently waits for us, offering us time, help, and opportunities to change and make progress on our journey to salvation."* Yet Pope Francis also warns against presumption. The gardener's mercy is not a free pass to avoid repentance. It is an invitation to take seriously the fleeting nature of our lives and the urgency of conversion. We cannot remain barren trees forever; our faith must become fruitful through acts of love, forgiveness, and service.

Lent invites us to meditate on the Four Last Things: death, judgment, heaven, and hell. These realities remind us that our time on earth is limited, and our choices have eternal consequences. The parable of the fig tree brings this into sharp focus. If we fail to bear fruit, we risk being "cut down."

This is not meant to terrify us into submission but to awaken us to the profound seriousness of our calling as Christians. Our ultimate concern must be the salvation of our souls and the souls of those entrusted to us. Lent is the perfect time to evaluate our spiritual lives and make the necessary changes to align ourselves with God's will.

So how do we ensure that we bear fruit? Perhaps we can think about this in three ways:

1. Cultivate the Soil: Spend time in prayer, particularly meditating on Scripture, which nourishes the soul.
2. Fertilize with Grace: Frequent the sacraments, especially confession and the Eucharist, which give us the grace to grow in holiness.
3. Prune What is Dead: Identify habits of sin and work to eliminate them.

4. Bear Fruit in Charity: Let your repentance manifest in acts of love—serving others, forgiving those who have hurt you, and living out the Beatitudes.

In his 2013 homily on this Gospel, Francis said: *"God is a Father who always waits for us. He waits for us, never tires of forgiving us if we turn to Him with a contrite heart."* This divine patience is at the heart of Lent. God's mercy gives us the opportunity to change, but it is not an excuse for complacency. The barren tree cannot rely on the gardener's mercy forever. The time to respond is now. Saint Thomas Aquinas reminds us that God's justice and mercy meet perfectly in Christ. As we reflect on this Gospel, let us hear the voice of the merciful gardener calling us to repentance. Let us not waste the time we have been given but respond to God's grace with open hearts, striving to bear fruit in our lives.

Fourth Sunday of Lent

Once again, we come to the most famous of all of the parables of Our Lord in Saint Luke's Gospel, that of the Prodigal Son. No less than Charles Dickens declared this as the greatest short story ever written. No doubt, we are all very familiar with the story, perhaps etched in our minds through the stunning painting of Rembrandt van Rijn's classic "The Return of the Prodigal Son."

Even if we ourselves have never seen the actual masterpiece itself in the Hermitage Museum in Saint Petersburg, Russia, we know it through the image which was hung in countless Churches in the 1990s and early '00's, most especially due to the spiritual devotion to it, which Fr. Henri Nouwen's spiritual book, *The Return of the Prodigal Son: A Story of Homecoming* (1992), offered to the world.

Yes, for my generation of priests, going to Cathedral Seminary in Douglaston from 1990-1994 and at the Pontifical North American College in Rome from 1994-1999 as a seminarian, the image of Rembrandt's "The Return of the Prodigal Son" was a constant image for reflection.

In fact, when I was assigned to teach full-time in 2004 at the high school seminary, the then Cathedral Preparatory Seminary, now Cathedral Prep High School and Seminary, the image of the Prodigal Son was prominent in the chapel of the high school.

Yes, I would dare say that most of us, due to homilies over the years from priests and deacons, are very familiar with Rembrandt's painting, with the two rather distinct hands, one more masculine and the other more feminine, perhaps representing the all-embracing love of God the Father.

What I would like to propose today for our reflection is the absolute radicality of the parable of the Prodigal Son. Even if we were to describe it as the parable of the angry brother, or perhaps more common, the patient and loving father, it is a powerful parable. Yes, as the U.S. Roman Catholic author from the southern part of our nation, Flannery O'Connor, states, "to the hard of hearing you shout, and for the almost blind you draw large and startling figures" (Flannery O'Connor, *Mysteries and Manners: Occasional Prose*, selected and edited by Sally and Robert Fitzgerald; New York: Farrar, Straus and Giroux; 1969, pages 33-34).

This parable is meant to cause us not to smile benignly, but to be openly shocked. It is meant to knock us down to our knees and make us realize some powerful lessons, which the great theologian and Catholic apologist of the new media, Bishop Robert E. Barron, has already articulated (and I apologize to the Bishop, as I am freely adapting them, while still trying to remain faithful to his message!): first, to recognize and find your center; second, to recognize that one is a sinner; and third, to know that life is not about you!

Ultimately, this path to spiritual growth, which Bishop Barron describes as the "Strangest Way," is all about two things: first, perceiving, not just seeing; and second, triumphing over one's own intrinsic selfishness.

Like the son who abandons his father's house, how often do you and I just see what's right in front of us and not really perceive? How often are we able to look beyond the externals, what is immediately available to our senses, to see how the immanent Lord of all creation, of all reality, is really in our midst?

The son who says no to his father's wishes disappears to a far-off land, and, due to his own pride, due to his own shortsightedness, finds a place with the pigs. To be with the pigs, the most unclean of all the animals of God's creation, according to the Hebraic Law, would be the ultimate insult to a son of Israel. The fact that he would, as we are told in Luke's Gospel, long to even taste the food that is given to the pigs should tell us how far he has descended.

And yet, into the picture, comes Jesus the Christ. He is God, and yet he empties himself and takes the form of a servant, being born in the likeness of men. Like the son in the parable, Our Blessed Lord allows himself to experience all the humiliations of being human. He knows our hunger, our thirst, our longing for home and for security. He knows them and he embraces them, taking them into his Most Sacred Heart, wounded for our offenses, which also knows his every little suffering. We can be sure that we can unite our suffering to his, our sufferings, whether large or small, whether profound or mundane. Jesus the Christ knows the abandonment of the Prodigal Son, not due his own personal circumstances, but out of love for us, his sinful brothers and sisters.

As to the second point, it is necessary for us to grasp in this parable the necessity for our own triumph over selfishness. For the Prodigal Son, the father in this parable, and the ego-wounded older brother, it is all a matter of triumphing over all of own intrinsic selfishness. Each of us, no matter how altruistic we might be, suffers from one nagging, one consistent question- "how does this affect me?" We worry about our status, our place, our "rights," and how we might be hurt. And yet, the Lord Jesus is the Lord of Mercy. He works in a way in which we truly do not understand. If God's nature is Love, then Mercy is the concrete application of that Love who God is, and Justice is the correct application of who and what God is. Each of the main characters in this parable teach us this truth, namely that it is necessary for each and every one of us to "get over ourselves" to see the movements of God, the All-Merciful One, in our lives.

When we hear this parable of the Prodigal Son, one which we might be all too familiar with in our hearts and minds, may we listen with eyes open to see the shocking big letters of this parable and with ears eager to hear the screaming message of God the Eternal Lover whose mercy knows no bounds and whose justice, even though it may seem foreign to our experience, knows the reality of God who loves us.

Annunciation

In the northern Italian city of Padua, Enrico Scrovegni, a wealthy landowner, built a chapel on his property in order to ask Almighty God for forgiveness for the sin of usury (lending money out for interest). Scrovegni constructed the chapel in a grand, ornate style that caused some in the neighboring monastery to think it garish. He hired one of the finest artists of his day, Giotto (Ambrogio Bondone, 1267–1337), to paint elaborate frescoes about the life of Jesus Christ and His Blessed Mother, Mary.

Among the first in a series is a famous one of the Annunciation, which we read about in the Gospel pericope given to us in the liturgy for this Solemnity of the Annunciation of the Blessed Virgin Mary from the Evangelist Luke. The Angel Gabriel, in this famous painting, is to the left bringing the Good News to the Blessed Virgin Mary, who sits at the right in a remarkably beautiful manner, signifying openness and receptivity.

This famous fresco of the Annunciation has shaped much of the Western world's visual understanding of this key event in the history of salvation, Whether we know the name of Giotto or not, most of us probably have the image of the winged archangel appearing before Our Lady, telling her that she will conceive and bear a child who will be named Jesus. Even in my grade school Nativity play back in 1983, that's how the scene was set. (I was chosen by my teacher at Holy Name School in Brooklyn to play Saint Joseph. This was the pinnacle of my acting career.)

An alternate way of thinking about the Annunciation that has always shaped my visualization of this great and joyful mystery comes from Franco Zeffirelli's *Jesus of Nazareth* (1977). In this stunning film, Olivia Hussey portrays the Blessed Mother. In the scene of the Annunciation, we see no angel and we do not hear any heavenly voices. All we see is the remarkably expressive eyes of the beautiful actress who speaks aloud to someone or something that we cannot see. Her eyes tell the entire story — not only fear, surprise, apprehension, but also remarkable openness and burning, intense love for God and the things of God.

The Blessed Virgin Mary, in the Gospel passage, in Giotto's fresco, and in Zeffirelli's film, shows remarkable receptivity. Our Lady had no concept of what would be happening to her. Probably the day of the Annunciation was to be a day like any other ordinary day. No one would have ever guessed that this would be one of the key days in the history of the universe. Mary is presented with a remarkable gift and with a remarkable challenge. Obviously, as the Evangelist expresses so well in the Gospel, perplexity reigned. Perhaps Our Lady thought: "Why me? Is this for real? Should I say yes?" Her "yes" continues the plan of salvation that was begun long ago. The Word of God that has existed from all eternity, conceived in the mutual, self-giving love of the Triune Godhead, continues in the Virgin womb of her who is the Immaculate Conception.

So, a question for us then: are we open, attentive, reasonable, and loving before God's plan in our lives? Do we listen in discernment of spirits for the message that God wishes to grant us? Would we have been able to reply as Mary did, despite her fear and anxiety? Mary is the model of openness for each and every one of us as Christians. She gives birth to the Eternal Son of the Father. Her intimate relationship with the Trinity allows us to call her, not only the Daughter of God the Father, not only the Mother of Christ, not only the Spouse of the Holy Spirit, but truly the Mother of God. On this feast day of the Virgin of Guadalupe, may all of us, women and men, married and single, clergy, religious, or laity, be able to give birth to Christ by our openness to the plan of God for our lives. Things are tough and may at times even seem impossible, but we need not fear — "For nothing is impossible for God." (Luke 1:37)

Saint Joseph

Today, we reflect on Saint Joseph, the silent figure whose faith, obedience, and humility shaped the course of salvation history. In his life, we see how God works through human instruments to fulfill His divine plan. Saint Joseph's witness is a profound reminder of what it means to live in faith, trust, and action.

The first reading from 2 Samuel reminds us of God's promise to King David: a lineage that would bring forth the Messiah. Saint Joseph stands as the custodian of this promise. As a descendant of David, he became the earthly father of Jesus, fulfilling God's covenant.

Sacred art has often portrayed Joseph in the background, holding a carpenter's tool or cradling the Christ Child. One striking example is *Guido Reni's "Saint Joseph with the Infant Jesus,"* where Joseph's protective embrace speaks volumes about his silent yet steadfast guardianship. His humility mirrors the divine paradox: God often works through the lowly to bring about His kingdom.

Saint Paul, in the letter to the Romans, describes Abraham's unwavering faith in God's promises. Joseph shares in this legacy of faith. Though Scripture records no words from Joseph, his actions speak loudly.

When faced with the extraordinary—Mary's pregnancy by the Holy Spirit—he chooses faith over doubt, obedience over self-will. Pope Francis, in *Patris Corde* (*With a Father's Heart*), calls Joseph "a man of creative courage." Like Abraham, Joseph trusted in the impossible, becoming an instrument of grace for the entire world.

Joseph's faith is akin to the quiet but powerful harmony in sacred music, such as Franz Schubert's *Ave Maria,* which conveys profound reverence and trust in divine providence without unnecessary flourish.

Saint Thomas Aquinas teaches that virtue is perfected in action. Joseph exemplifies this in the Gospel from Matthew, where he receives and obeys God's will through dreams. Despite fear, he takes Mary as his wife and provides Jesus with a home and a name.

Joseph's prudence guided him to discern God's will. His justice ensured that Mary and Jesus received the care and protection they needed. His fortitude carried him through trials like the flight into Egypt. Each virtue shines in Joseph, making him a model for every Christian who seeks to live a life of holiness.

In sacred art, this balance of action and contemplation is beautifully captured in *Georges de La Tour's "The Dream of Saint Joseph,"* where Joseph is bathed in divine light, attentive to the angel's message. The painting invites us to trust, like Joseph, in the quiet yet transformative whispers of God.

Saint Joseph's life challenges us to trust God amid uncertainties. Like him, we are called to respond to God's plans with faith and courage. As Pope Francis reflects, Joseph's silence is not passivity but active listening—a disposition of openness to God's voice.

We can also see Joseph as a patron of workers and families, reminding us of the dignity of labor and the sanctity of family life. His role as a foster father speaks to the beauty of spiritual fatherhood, a gift that transcends biology.

As we meditate on the life of Saint Joseph, let us seek his intercession. Let his humility inspire our actions, his faith strengthen our trust in God, and his obedience guide our discernment.

Through sacred art, sacred music, and the timeless teachings of the Church, we glimpse Joseph's greatness—not in grandeur but in the quiet, faithful fulfillment of God's will. May we, like Joseph, embrace the call to be silent yet steadfast guardians of Christ in our own lives.

Palm Sunday of the Lord's Passion

As many of you e might know, this liturgy which we celebrate today is a rather odd one. Prior to the reforms of the Sacred Liturgy called for by the Second Vatican Council (1962-1965), Catholics around the world would have celebrated two separate Sundays — one which would have been "Passion Sunday," in which we as a Church would have commemorated the dolorous Passion and life-giving death of our Savior Christ, and another one the following week in which we would have celebrated the Lord's triumphant entry into Jerusalem and the beginning of Holy Week. By 1960, with Pope St. John XXIII's liturgical reforms, we would have had the Passion Sunday be known as "First Sunday of the Lord's Passion" and Palm Sunday be called "Second Sunday of the Passion or Palm Sunday."

Now, with this liturgical reform over the past fifty or so years since the liturgical reforms called by Pope St. Paul VI, we have these two separate Sundays, one filled with pain and sorrow (Passion Sunday) and the other with an abundance of hope, joy, and expectation (Palm Sunday) combined into one. The current sacred liturgy recognizes this well and allows for it with its two Gospels, one for the Procession of Palms and one (which is generally in most parish churches and chapels read as a dialogue) about the Passion of the Lord.

Although some may decry this joining together of these two Sundays as a quasi-manic emotional roller-coaster ride, I most certainly do not. I truly believe that this Sunday, this "Palm Sunday of the Lord's Passion" is the most proper representation of the

Christian life which we could have presented to us liturgically. It is a Sunday of highs and lows, of joy and sorrows, of cheers and tears, and, if we are honest with ourselves, isn't that the way our lives really are?

No one is happy 24 hours a day, seven days a week, 365 days of the year. We all have our crescendos (our highs) and our diminuendos (our lows.) We all have the moments where we feel like we're on top of the world, living our best lives, and, in the next few moments, due to circumstance beyond our control (or even sometimes because of our own fault,) we have a crashing fall.

This Palm Sunday which we celebrate today is one of great joy. Jesus of Nazareth is rightly recognized as the one, true Christ, the long-awaited Messiah. This Passion Sunday which we celebrate today is one of great sorrow. The All-Beautiful One is scarred. He is broken, bloodied, beaten, struck down for our sins, his glorious countenance marred beyond all semblance of recognition. The only innocent one is unjustly condemned, bearing the weight of our sins. Yet, in all of this, there is no real contradiction in celebrating these two events on the same liturgical day.

For this is our life as human beings in this veil of tears. We live in a fallen world, one which suffers under the weight of the fall, of the original sin of our first parents, Adam and Eve, as well as our own personal sin. Yet still, we can laugh, we can cheer, we can experience the love of another human being, the smile and the personal encounter in which we can know we are, in a limited, human way, the love of the transcendent God. Every day in the life of a Christian is Palm Sunday because every day is filled with the joy of the Lord. Every day in the life of a Christian is Passion Sunday because as the music group REM sang many years ago, "everybody hurts."

However, the Palms and the Passion both lead to the glory of what we know is true above anything else — the Lord's Resurrection, his triumph over sin and death. Thank God for the Church in her wisdom acknowledging the truth that each day for us in our lives is filled with passion and palms.

Evening Mass of the Lord's Supper

This evening, we proclaim the Gospel according to Saint John. Saint John's is the most sophisticated of all the Gospels, linguistically, philosophically, and theologically. Like Mark's Gospel, it has no infancy narrative; there is no story of the birth of Christ. Instead, it is set up completely differently from all of the other Gospels.

Matthew, Mark, and Luke are what we call Synoptic Gospels. The word "synoptic" is Greek, meaning "to look together," and indeed that is the case in these three Gospels. All three more or less follow a similar structure. John's Gospel is an entirely different creature. It starts, not with a genealogy of Jesus' human ancestry, like Matthew and Luke, but with a beautiful, poetic prologue, set in the vastness of all eternity.

It is very different from the beginning of Mark's Gospel, which is so blunt and direct. Why is this Gospel so different from the others? Like each of the others, John's was written in a particular time period and for a particular audience; yet, it is also different because it reflects one of the first times that the Church used not just the language, but also the style, of another culture. It is Hellenic, or Greek, in its style.

The Gospel is traditionally broken into two parts — chapters 1–11 are called the Book of Signs, while chapters 12–21 are called the Book of Glory. I particularly love praying with the Book of Signs. In John's Gospel, there is a particular word for what in the other Gospels are called miracles. In John, we call them "signs." For the sake of simplicity, I'll suffice it to say that each sign, each of the acts that Jesus performs in this first part of John's Gospel, gets bigger and bigger — each one pointing to the reality that is right in front of the people of Jesus' day — namely, that this man is the Messiah. From the Wedding Feast at Cana, to the various healings performed by the Lord, to the crucial moment in the Bread of Life discourse where Jesus sets forth a radical truth and loses so many of his followers, to where all these signs culminate — in the raising of Lazarus. It is in this chapter that we see the Lord Jesus at his most human, in weeping deeply for his friend, Lazarus, and at his most divine (until, of course, we read of his own resurrection), in raising Lazarus, who was four days dead, to life.

The chapters that comprise what is called the Book of Glory give us the story of the Lord's Paschal Mystery — his passion, death, and resurrection — beginning with the Last Supper. In the Last Supper, John emphasizes the washing of the feet — though, recall he also includes the Bread of Life discourse earlier in the Gospel, where he gives us a rich, beautiful theology of the Eucharist.

So, when encounter the Lord Jesus this evening, we are already in the midst of the Book of Glory. We join the Lord Jesus and his Apostles in the cenacle, that furnished upper room. And we encounter them in medias res, in the midst of the action, the action being the *mandatum.* We need not worry about whether the Last Supper was the Paschal meal or not (as many biblical scholars do), because either way, his Passion is His passing over to the Father. Whether the date of the Pasch fell on the dinner (the prototype of the prolongation of His Sacrifice until the end of time) or on His actual death, the message, the truth, and the reality is the same.

In John 13:1, notice the word "knew." The verse reads: "Jesus knew that his hour had come to pass from this world to the Father. He loved his own in the world and he loved them to the end." What does this mean? Basically, in His humanity, this is an awareness of His origin and His destiny with the Father. We clearly have the expression that this supper was the expression of His Passover to the Father. So, in the *Mandatum,* the Lord Jesus performs the gesture of a slave. The King of the Universe, the Brightness of the Father's Glory, the Word made Flesh, gets down on his hands and knees and bathes the filthy, dirty, grimy feet of his disciples. In the eyes of this world,

He performs a gesture of the slave. The Lord Jesus anticipates His passion and makes His disciples enter also into this dynamic of service. He truly reveals God in this act of love, for God is love, and this love is a gift. Jesus saves by diminishing Himself.

And even though it is not covered, but as I mentioned, it is assumed, as the Johannine Eucharistic Theology is covered in John 6 (in the Book of Signs), we then move to the central mystery of the most holy evening, the institution of the Eucharist. The various synoptic gospels emphasized different elements such as "eat and drink," "for many," "for you," the elevation of the chalice, the intention of the sacrifice for the forgiveness of sins, the formation of a new covenant, and doing this in the memory of Jesus. However, for our sake, we need to recognize that this Eucharistic institution is full of divine prerogatives.

The nucleus of these records is that, within a Hebraic meal, Jesus changes the significance of the Jewish prayers within their meals. With Him, the bread and wine become the symbols of His body and blood offered on the cross. In the words of consecration, we find a fourth announcement of the Passion. In the statement, "I will not drink of it again until I drink it anew in my Father's kingdom" there is a new announcement of the Resurrection. Matthew alone uses the words "eat" and "drink," and he alone shows the object of the shedding of blood, forgiveness of sins. Luke has "for many;" Luke and Paul alone have "chalice," "do this," and body "given for you."

Because of the assumed power of His words, they are sacramental and effective. Cyril of Jerusalem describes a "mystical exchange," Ambrose speaks of the conversion of the elements, Aquinas and the Council of Trent of transubstantiation. This is the same reality, but we use different terms showing the development of doctrine. Jesus says blood shed for many or all; He claims to offer atonement on behalf of all, assuming it can be effective for all people. This Son of Man assumes the ability to take away sins. This Son of God announces a new Covenant, which only God can do. "Do this in Memory of me"; they are within the Passover, which recalls the Exodus. The Lord seems to substitute a memorial of Himself. He becomes sacramentally present in the form of bread and wine, the most common staples of the diet of the common person of Jesus' day. In the institution of the Eucharist, <u>Jesus saves by diminishing Himself.</u>

The third central mystery on which we reflect this holy evening is the institution of the ministerial priesthood. We read about this more in John 17, with the Lord's famous prayer of "Ut Unum Sint." The Lord Jesus, the true and eternal priest, whose one single sacrifice on the altar, reveal Him to the priest, the altar, and the Lamb of Sacrifice, knows His Apostles, for he himself has called each and every one of them by name. He knows them inside and out, the virtues and the vices which each of them possesses. He knows the one who will betray Him and he knows the one to whom His Blessed Mother will be entrusted. He knows the one who will deny him three times before the cock crows twice, the one to whom He will entrust His

Mystical Body, His Bride, the Church, the People of God. In His sharing of the priesthood, in His call with a "brother's love," the Lord Jesus, the one, true High Priest, continues to save and sanctify the world. In the institution of the ministerial priesthood, <u>Jesus saves by diminishing Himself.</u>

We see next the actions in the Garden, where the New Adam reverses the action of the Old Adam's action in the Garden, we see that in the midst of all who abandon Jesus, the Son of Man is the one who abides; Jesus, the Lord, the Son of God, remains. He does the same today, in all the tabernacles around the world (now emptied for this Evening Mass of the Lord's Supper) in the Eucharist. In the Garden, <u>Jesus saves by diminishing Himself.</u>

With this in mind, how can we then react to these mysteries which we explore and celebrate this holy evening. Namely this, by <u>diminishing ourselves</u>, no matter what our state in the Christian life.

Bishop Robert Barron, in his text, *Catholicism: A Journey into the Heart of the Faith* (2011) describes Saint Therese of Lisieux's particularly unique role as a Doctor of the Church and as a saint. Barron describes Therese's sanctity as a "transfigured prudence," and he goes on to state: "…for at the heart of the little way is the capacity to know in any given situation the precise demand of love, how best in. the here and now of the present moment to will the good of the other." (210)

And, isn't that the case, ultimately with love? Isn't that what another Doctor like Therese stated in the *Summa theologiae, prima secunda*, and quoted in *The Catechism of the Catholic Church* (1766). The Catechism goes on to say, citing yet another Doctor, Augustine, concerning love: "All other affections have their source in this first movement of the human heart toward the good. Only the good can be loved."

Only the good can be loved. One of the most important lessons that Therese can teach us is that, in order to truly love, we must triumph over our individual passions, conquering our own sinful, fallen inclination of our own needs and selfishness to put others first, to, ultimately, put Christ first.

Allow me to illustrate this from a moment in Therese's life from her childhood. On Christmas Day 1886, Therese, whom we know was a tremendously emotional and neurotic child (some now claiming she suffered from Attachment Anxiety Disorder), was excited to have her father place, as was the custom in the Martin family, little gifts in her shoes. As the young Therese went up the stairs on Christmas Day, having received her little trinkets in her shoes, thinking she was out of earshot, her now Sainted father, Louis, commented to her sister: "Well, fortunately, this is the last year." Therese, upon hearing the comment, had to make a decision- to grow in sorrow and despair, to grow in anger and rage, to the words uttered by her father, or to react by not taking offense, by responding in love, and to not ruin the family's Christmas with a fit or a tantrum. This seemingly unimportant event and Therese's reaction to it was viewed by the Little Flower as the Lord breaking into her heart, assisting her to learn how to love.

In this little Christmas Day drama, Therese is able to begin to will the good of another, to break free of her burning compulsion to place her ego, her needs first, before the needs of her family. This is the beginning of the "Little Way" in her life. Pray that each of us in our lives can learn to follow the "Little Way," to learn to love by conquering our own innate selfishness and ego and to heed the words of this Doctor of the Church from the 11th chapter of *Story of a Soul*: "O my God, Thou knowest I have never desired but to love Thee alone. I seek no other glory. Thy Love has gone before me from my childhood, it has grown with my growth, and now it is an abyss the depths of which I cannot fathom."

Good Friday

Some believe that Judas betrayed Christ because he, in a misguided way, wanted to help Jesus "clear the air" with the Jewish authorities and thus be able to get his message out even further. Others posit that Judas was possessed by the Devil. We read that Satan "entered him." Did he have free will? Some have speculated that all this is part of a grand scheme of events, all part of the plan and Judas was just playing his part in the vast cosmic drama. Still others have the thought that Judas was just trying to force Jesus to take a stand, that he was disillusioned by Jesus' slow pace and focus on the world to come rather than the revolutionary actions that this zealot wanted. A few, in a rather odd way of thinking, seem to imply that the Lord Jesus wished Judas to betray him so that all this lead to the events of the Passion, Death and Resurrection. And there's those who take the story on face value and hold that love of money, pure and simple greed for those thirty pieces of silver, was at the cause of Judas' actions. Perhaps the most radical interpretation I had ever come across held that Judas had been simply a representative character, someone who represented the people of Israel of Jesus' day. So much for contemporary scholarship.

Frankly, in some of these accounts from exegetes, theologians, and spiritual writers, Judas comes across as almost a victim of circumstance who just had the whole situation get out of hand. Why did he do it? Maybe he just was greedy; personally, I think we'll never know the whole situation and I don't believe that we really need to know why he did it. This is not said to mitigate the betrayal of Jesus with a kiss. What we do need to know for certain is THAT he betrayed the Lord. What we do need to know for certain is THAT he sinned and turned away from the Lord. We need to know THAT he was the agent who handed He who is truth, goodness, beauty and love incarnate to the hands of sinful men. Why he did isn't as important as the fact that he did it.

The fact is, for all of us, that we all, each in our own way, sin. Each of us, in thought, word and deed, betray the Lord who loves us by giving us life, who taught us through Sacred Scripture, through the unchanging Tradition of the Church and the Magisterium, and by whom we've been fed by his Real Presence in the Eucharist. We sin, sadly in great ways, by mortal sins and in little ways by venial sins. We sin by our personal actions and by our cooperation in social sin, the prevailing attitude of this world that leads to the culture of death. We sin in our actions and our attitudes. All of us, especially those of us who share in Sacred Orders and those of you configured to Christ as his Spouse in consecrated life need to recognize this sad reality.

We have two options, then, on this Good Friday. We can survey that wonderous cross and we can shiver with despair and that is a logical reaction. All too often in our lives, we are like Judas, and, in our sins, betray the Lord. We, by our sins, hammer down the nails into his hands and feet; we, by our sins, crown the King of the Universe not with many crowns, but with thistles and thorns; we, by our sins, thrust the spear into his side, forgoing all too often the blood and water which flow from his side, the fountain of sacramental life, and instead can just be satisfied with the bitter gall that this world serves up time and again.

And it is good to stand in fear and trembling of the cross of Christ. But never, ever, gaze on the cross in despair. For, as we will sing in just a few moments, the salvation of the world has hung there and the tree of shame has become the tree of victory.

At its root, sin is a three-fold alienation from God, others and our own self. What we need then to battle this alienation is a three-fold reconciliation that can only come from one who is like us in all things but sin and one who is also fully divine. It can only come in and through the Lord Jesus, true man and true God.

Our lack of basic integrity has to be healed. Jesus is the one who opens His arms wide on the cross in an embrace of love for you and me. Through His action of total self-giving, He conquers sin and death to bring us to new life.

When we look on this cross, we do so in awe and say: "*O Crux ave, spes unica, hoc Passionis tempore! piis adauge gratiam, reisque dele criminal,*" which roughly translates as "O hail the cross our only hope in this passiontide grant increase of grace to believers and remove the sins of the guilty."

However, the good news is that, once we recognize our sin, we have no need for the despair that overtook Judas. We have the power of the Sacrament of Reconciliation, of having our souls cleansed, shriven of the dirt and defilement of sin. The Cross today then stands as the Mirror of Truth. May our veneration, our kiss, of the cross of Christ today not be like that of Judas, but that of Mary, the Mother of Mercy, who kept station at her Son's cross. May we not be like Judas and fall into despair when we recognize, when we acknowledge our sins but as Saint Francis De Sales urges us: "Do not be disheartened by your imperfections, but always rise up with fresh courage" and may we, in our lives, continue to be the mercy of God in the midst of the misery of mankind.

The Easter Vigil

An important lesson to learn this evening, is patience. One of the things we can learn about God from the readings we proclaim this evening which take us through salvation history is that we have a God who cooks with a crockpot, not with a microwave. We have a God who takes his time, who allows for human freedom and with it, the mistakes and sins we commit, a God who gives us time to repent and turn to him, a God whose love for us transcends even death itself. Simply put, God is patient. Salvation history teaches us that fact.

God is patient. I know that I am not. I would have scrapped everything if I were the creator and started on a new project right after Adam and Eve's fall. I would have been so hurt by the lack of faith shown by the Israelites in the desert; I would have been so dumbfounded by the lack of trust in the people of Israel and the need for the prophets to arise to keep them on task and faithful. I would have been one who would have liked the three days in the tomb to be three minutes and I would have been the apostle to have asked the Lord in his earthly life reveal his plan to me so that I could make my own plans around it.

I am not patient, and I used to be worse, especially in my years of teaching high school, but I'm trying to be more and more; I believe that my lack of patience is all part of a desire to control because at my essence, I am a person who, if left to his own devices, would be a big, frenetic ball of chaos.

But thanks be to God, that he is patient, merciful, and kind. Easter shows us the patience of the Lord. The fact is, the Lord's cooking with a crockpot, marinating, letting things sit! This is so apparent.

Patience, so apparent in our God this evening: St. Thomas Aquinas, stated that patience is attached to fortitude because it helps us to resist giving way to sadness, and to bear up under the difficulties of life with a certain equanimity or steadiness of soul. By it, we do not give way easily to emotional sadness or excessive anger, just like Jesus faced his passion. He suffered, but he never despaired. This is the way of God the Father, as demonstrated in his loving, providential care of us. This is the way of the Lord Jesus, as demonstrated in his most sorrowful, yet glorious and life giving. This is the way of the Holy Spirit, the bond of love and knowledge that exists between the Father and the Son from all eternity.

Patience, as I understand it, is an act of fortitude, since it helps us to endure painful or difficult things without weakening in our faith or our commitment to the truth. With patience, we are steady in the face of the annoyances and contradictions of life. Look to God the Father in the readings; look to his Son, Jesus, our Lord, God the Father puts up with his people, who time and again betray him, turn their back on him, are so willing to worship false gods, so eager to take the easy way out. Look to God the Son, who was born, well, to die, to save us from our sins. A single drop of blood from a prick of the finger of the Lord would have been enough to save us; and yet, our Lord, ever the extravagant lover, says that it is not enough. Like Flannery O'Connor, the great American Roman Catholic writer, who explains why she uses grotesque, so that the blind may see and the deaf may hear, Jesus, in his Passion, Death, and Resurrection, goes over the top for us. He loves us, beautifully, personally, passionately. He is enthralled with us, captivated by our beauty, he who is the all-beautiful one. He never wants us to want for anything, so he opens up his arms on the cross in an embrace of love for us, demonstrating his complete, utter, total self-giving, He wants to give us everything, and, because he loves us and cares for us, he is willing to let us not choose him and to do our own thing.

This brings us to the second aspect: perseverance. The readings on this most Holy Night tell us that God is willing to go the distance with us, and, because he is God, who can neither deceive or be deceived, we should too. Patience and suffering are often necessary acts of fortitude; they require great strength and brave endurance. Jesus says in John 16:33, "In this world you shall have tribulation, but have courage, I have overcome the world." The Resurrection of Christ from the dead proves this.

In this night of Easter joy, with our hearts filled with the *Risum Paschalum*, the Easter Laugh, as Christ Jesus bests Satan's pride through his patience and perseverance, may we have the courage and strength to imitate Christ, the patience one, the persevering one, the risen one. To him be glory and honor, now and forever. Amen

Easter Sunday

I had the opportunity to teach in the pre-theology program in the college seminary in Douglaston, New York, for a few years, while I was also teaching full-time in our High School Seminary. I looked forward to my weekly class very much, as it gave me a break from being the watchdog in a classroom full of teenagers. I was teaching one semester a class entitled "Jesus and the Gospels"- a course in biblical Christology. One day in class the pericope, we proclaim this morning came up, and I began to explain what some scholars speculate as the "Peter-John" rivalry. Some people posit that there was a rivalry between the disciples of Peter and the disciples of John. This idea was met with some upset by my students, but I kind of think it might be useful for us to explore this idea.

The contents of the Gospel of Mark are traditionally traced to Peter, (meaning he was Mark's source). John is attributed to John, and I do consider John to be the "Beloved Disciple," and the "Eyewitness" about whom we hear in the Fourth Gospel. I'm not suggesting that Peter wrote Mark, but because of Peter's relationship to Mark, I'll consider his perspective similar to Peter's.

Because of the difference in what details of gospel events are included or omitted in Mark and John, it can seem that there was a rivalry between Peter and John (or at least their disciples). Mark tends to include information that could slightly embarrass John. Note that Mark mentions a considerably embarrassing moment for John where he and his brother ask to sit at Jesus' right and left hand. When they try to get Jesus to agree to their request before they tell him what it is "'Teacher, we want you to do for us whatever we ask of You.'" John and James can seem a little bit like brats! Jesus makes this into a teaching moment at the expense of John's pride. This section is left out of John, I might add!

John, on the other hand, includes details that embarrass Peter and omits details that embarrass John. For instance, Mark's gospel does not name the Apostle who draws his sword and strikes the high priest's slave John is sure to mention that this Apostle who acted so rashly and against the wishes of his master was none other than Peter. And there are many other examples to which we could look!

Peter and John were the number one and number two disciples. They were part of Jesus' inner group. And yet, Peter and John, as we know, played very different roles in the life of Jesus. It was the two of them, along with James who were present at the Transfiguration and the resurrection of Jairus' daughter; they were also the ones Jesus requested to stay awake with him to pray in Gethsemane. James, being John's brother, may have simply been John's tag-along at these events.

Please note that in the Gospel passage we proclaim this morning, John is very careful to mention that John (mentioned as "the other disciple") beat Peter to the tomb in their foot race. John 20: states: "So Peter and the other disciple went forth, and they were going to the tomb. The two were running together; and the other disciple ran ahead faster than Peter and came to the tomb first" We know, of course, from our Catholic tradition, that this is representative of authority, as represented by Peter, and love, as represented by John, as having their respective places in the life of the Christian.

A question then about the moral implications of the resurrection for the Christian life- how can we get along with, relate to, and truly love our brothers and sisters whom we encounter daily? We, by and large, do not get to choose the individuals with whom we spend our days. And, by and large, we all have the best intentions; we all have the same ideals. It's in the living out of those ideals, the living out daily of our baptismal charism, it's in the character flaws of others, in those little areas in ourselves, our failure of self-realization that can lead to dilemmas. It's when we allow annoyances to grow into resentments, and then the resentments fester into a much bigger deal than they need to be. Drama, too much drama!

We can remember, especially when we are annoyed or angry, that people are generally good. Listen to the words of Pope Francis: "From my point of view, God is the light that illuminates the darkness, even if it does not dissolve it, and a spark of divine light is within each of us." Recognize the presence of God within us.

Can we see each of our brothers and sisters not as competition for the top spot, not as annoyances, but as they are truly meant to be seen, as someone who is precisely our brother, someone who is in our life as a blessing? Peter and John could and did, especially after the resurrection of the Lord and Savior, Jesus Christ. Two different men, two different personalities, two different styles of living out their apostolic callings, but one heart, one mind- the mind of Christ Jesus.

Second Sunday of Easter

Divine Mercy Sunday

Imagine what it must have been like for the Apostles. Just imagine what it would have been like for them, hiding in that room, in the days after the passion, the death, and the resurrection of our Lord Jesus. The reports were coming in, from Mary Magdalene, the apostle to the Apostles, that the Lord was risen, truly risen. Certainly, the Apostles were, no doubt, overjoyed with this news. But, I bet that, mixed in with that joy, was also a certain amount of fear, a little bit of apprehension. After all, what would Jesus say to them? I mean, each of the Apostles, in their own ways, betrayed Jesus. It wasn't just Judas, who sold the Lord out and then despaired. It wasn't just Peter, who explicitly denied even knowing the Lord Jesus three times. Every single one of them failed Jesus. In his hour of need, when he asked them to watch and pray with him was he underwent his agony in the garden, they couldn't even do that; they fell asleep. When the Lord was about to be taken away by the guards, they all scattered, like frightened children. In his passion on the Cross, only Beloved John and the women, his Blessed Mother, and the Magdalene remained.

Three long years they were with Jesus. The Word made flesh imparted to them the words of eternal life. These first priests of the New Covenant gathered with him in the Cenacle and were the first to receive the bread of life and chalice of salvation. And still, they failed. They ran. And now Jesus was back.

What would he do when he met them? Would he have righteous indignation? He had every right to say, "You all left me; You all abandoned me; How dare you?" And yet, when the Lord Jesus appears, he says four little words; when he stands in their midst, he says four very different words than what I would have said to these guys-Jesus, meek and humble of heart, Jesus, the just one, Jesus just looks at them, standing there in his glorified body and says to them, four little words: peace be with you. He says this for he is in their midst and he himself is peace. Jesus says this because he is the Divine Mercy. Mark's Gospel, which we proclaimed yesterday, tells us a little more bluntly, "He rebuked them for their lack of faith and for the hardness of heart in not believing those to whom he had appeared." But the Evangelists say absolutely nothing about any words of rebuke that the Lord Jesus could have said to Peter and the others about their abandonment of him. He forgives them.

The Lord's gift to us is his peace. It is part and parcel of the very nature of God as the Divine Mercy. Today, we celebrate that Divine Mercy in a special way as we conclude the Easter Octave. Mercy has become quite the catch phrase today. God bless the daughters of Venerable Catherine McAuley, our Religious Sisters of Mercy, who were into mercy before it became hip and cool.

Did you ever notice the cross that's worn by the Religious Sisters of Mercy of Alma, Michigan? The Mercy cross is a simple cross, made of black wood, on a simple black cord. In the center of the cross, in the midst of the black, is a smaller white cross. When I asked one of the Sisters to explain it to me, she mentioned that the white represents God's mercy in the midst of the black, which signifies the misery of humanity. The mercy of God in the midst of humanity's misery- that is the place that the Lord Jesus who is mercy made flesh is, and no more so than when he appears in his gloriously risen body.

What then is mercy? Mercy is the ability to see all with the eyes of Christ. It is recognizing all of us are creatures in the loving hand of the creature; it is recognizing the need in each and every one of us for the loving embrace of God. In Hebrew, a word that corresponds to mercy is hesed, God's loving kindness, his faithfulness. It is part of God's very nature and it is the foundation of the covenant. When we show mercy to others, we participate in the very life of God. Seeing with the eyes of mercy means to give practical assistance to all those in need.

The Lord's gift is peace. It is mercy, divine mercy. How can we show mercy to all those whom we encounter? How can we, each in our own vocations, clergy, religious, laity, and states in life, clerical, consecrated, married or single, be the mercy of God in the misery of mankind? We can start by examining ourselves, freeing ourselves from any and all grudges, past hurts, and resentments. This is not an easy process and, indeed, might not even be possible. Can we recognize that we have been hurt by others, and that hurt, which we can carry around with us for years, unless we let it go, addressing it if we can with the ones who have hurt us, if possible, or at least acknowledging it to ourselves when it cannot be possible? Can we acknowledge that we have hurt others, most of the time inadvertently perhaps, but we have caused hurt nonetheless, and deal with the fact that we need mercy and forgiveness too.

Four little words: "Peace be with you." Venerable Catherine McAuley writes: "The simplest and most practical lesson I know…is to resolve to be good today, but better tomorrow. Let us take one day only in hands, at a time, merely making a resolve for tomorrow, thus

we may hope to get on taking short, careful steps, not great strides."
Continue to take those short, careful steps, practically seeing Christ
and then being Christ to one another. This is the way of mercy.

Third Sunday of Easter

The readings today from Acts, Revelation, and John's Gospel reveal a powerful message of courage, praise, and the calling to follow Christ even in the face of difficulty.

In the passage from Acts, we find Peter and the apostles standing before the Sanhedrin, courageously proclaiming the name of Jesus despite orders to remain silent. When warned not to preach, Peter replies boldly, "We must obey God rather than men" (Acts 5:29). Despite facing persecution, they rejoiced, finding honor in being "found worthy to suffer dishonor for the sake of the name" (Acts 5:41). This is a profound example of courage and faithfulness, demonstrating how conviction in Christ gives us strength to stand firm even when it is difficult.

We may not face the same level of persecution, but we are still called to witness to Christ in our own lives, whether at work, in our communities, or with family. This might mean speaking out against injustice or simply sharing our faith with those around us. As St. John Paul II said, "Do not be afraid. Open wide the doors to Christ!" When we remain faithful, God will work through us.

The reading from Revelation offers a vision of heavenly worship, where "every creature in heaven and on earth and under the earth" praises the Lamb, Jesus Christ, who was slain. This scene is filled with joy and reverence, as countless angels cry out, "Worthy is the Lamb that was slain" (Revelation 5:12). This passage reminds us that worship is at the heart of our faith—joining our voices with the saints and angels in a continuous hymn of praise.

This vision encourages us to bring a heart of gratitude and worship into every part of our lives. Worship isn't confined to Mass; it's a way of life. Every act of love and every choice to follow God reflects the worship of heaven. As St. Augustine said, "Our hearts are restless until they rest in you, O Lord." When we live in worship, we are living for our true purpose, glorifying God in all things.

In the Gospel, Jesus appears to His disciples on the shore, after His resurrection, and offers them a miraculous catch of fish. He then turns to Peter and asks, "Do you love me?" three times. Each time Peter affirms his love, Jesus responds, "Feed my lambs" or "Tend my sheep." This scene is significant: Jesus restores Peter after his three-fold denial, giving him a renewed mission and calling to shepherd His people.

Just as Peter was asked to confirm his love and commitment, we too are called to renew our love and commitment to Christ. Each day, Christ asks us, "Do you love me?"—and we answer not only with words but with our actions. Loving Christ means caring for others, reaching out to those in need, and being a shepherd in our own sphere of influence, whether that's within our families, friendships, or community.

These readings remind us that following Christ requires courage, gratitude, and commitment. We might not face the Sanhedrin, but we all encounter moments that call for a choice: Will we stand for our faith? Will we live in gratitude, joining the worship of heaven? Will we answer Christ's call to love, even when it requires sacrifice?

In today's Eucharist, let us ask God to strengthen us with the same courage as Peter and the apostles, to fill our hearts with the praise of the Lamb, and to renew our commitment to love and serve Christ. May we live as bold witnesses to God's love, bringing His light to those around us.

Fourth Sunday of Easter

In the Diocese of Rome, this fourth Sunday of Easter is what traditionally is called "Good Shepherd Sunday." This is the Sunday when the Bishop of Rome, the Pope, ordains men to the priesthood.

In the past, under Pope St. John Paul II, for instance, this was a large number of men ordained to the priesthood, from religious orders as well as from dioceses all around the world, including, of course, men from the Diocese of Rome itself.

The image of the Good Shepherd is one that is naturally associated with the Lord Jesus, the One, True, High Priest, in whose priesthood all of us who are baptized share. But the Lord calls some men to serve in the ministerial priesthood, to be sacramentally ordained for service of God's Holy Church. This past year, when we read about the priesthood and the episcopacy in the press, the image that might be evoked is not necessarily that of the Good Shepherd, but that of the hired hand, the one who runs away when the sheep are threatened.

This sad reality is that the betrayal of the sacred office of Priesthood and Episcopacy by a few has tarnished the image of who and what the priest and bishop is called to be – the Good Shepherd whom the Lord describes in John's Gospel.

As a professor in a major seminary, I am edified by the selflessness of the men whom I encounter who are discerning their call to the priesthood. They are dedicated men, striving for holiness and integrity of life, and I truly believe that they will be godly men, in the best sense of that word, meaning this – men who have made God and His Church the center of their life. They will, in turn, be striving to be witnesses to the People of God of the Lord's presence in the world, leading them by preaching and teaching, caring for them by prudent care of the Church, and, most of all, sanctifying them through the administration of the sacraments. The priest is called to engage fully in the triple *munera* of the priesthood – to teach, to administer, and to sanctify. He is called to be the bearer of that gracious mystery who is God.

The Lord is still calling men to the priesthood, even in this age when the faults and sins of some priests have so clearly come to life. We are blessed with many programs to promote vocations to the priesthood. One essential element is the role of the family, that "first seminary," as Pope St. John Paul II called it in his document *Familaris Consortio*. We will have holy priests in the future if we have families that are encouraging and striving to be holy. We will have holy priests in the future if the parish, that essential seed-bed of faith, prays and encourages young men to truly consider a priestly vocation.

Above all, if we want vocations, we must have priests who are themselves happy, healthy and holy. In 1997, in an interview with U.S. Catholic, Bishop Robert E. Barron, then a professor at Mundelein Seminary in the Archdiocese of Chicago, was asked what a priestly vocation should look like. He responded: "A quick answer is someone of great soul. Someone who is magnanimous in the literal sense: magna anima, having a big soul. Someone who is in touch with human compassion, with love, with justice. Someone in touch with that deepest part of himself and others, and who lives and breathes the great culture that feeds the soul."

Twenty seven years after that interview, it is still true. We need men with great soul. The priest has to be the man who stands in the midst of the people with whom God has blessed him to serve as the model of the mystery bearer. Never lose sight that God himself is that gracious mystery. Father Barron in this interview continued, gave a practical example of how the priest is to live:

"To live a life of a mystery bearer is to make a commitment at the level of your behavior – your lifestyle and it involves those questions of celibacy and simplicity. It can't just be a disembodied intellectual exercise. It means I make a commitment of my life, and I'm going to live stubbornly in the presence of the mystery. That means attending to all that language about poverty and asceticism that the spiritual teachers insist upon."

The bishop who ordained me to priesthood was Thomas Vose Daily. He was a very large man and I still remember the sheer size of his hands when I placed them in his at my priestly ordination. The Bishop, a hockey and football player in his youth, enveloped my hands into his and asked if I promise respect and obedience to him and his successors. He then took the Oil of Chrism and drenched every single inch of my hands, consecrating my hands, setting them apart for the holy things for God's holy people. The Bishop time and again would reiterate to us seminarians, "Sometimes holiness is trying to be holy; sometimes the desire for prayer is prayer itself." If the priest wants to inspire more vocations to the priesthood, then he has to be striving for holiness himself.

On this Good Shepherd Sunday, pray for your shepherds, your priests and bishops, that they may indeed be good and holy and that, in their service to God's people, they may strive by words and deeds to sanctify the Bride of Christ, the Church, in the service of Christ, the Bridegroom.

Fifth Sunday of Easter

This Sunday's readings offer a powerful call to love, unity, and the new life that God is bringing forth. These passages are woven together with the message that, through love and discipleship, we become partakers in the renewal of the world and are transformed into a new creation in Christ.

In John's Gospel, Jesus gives His disciples a "new commandment": "Love one another. As I have loved you, so you also should love one another" (John 13:34). This call to love as Christ loved reaches its ultimate expression in His willingness to lay down His life. Saint Augustine once said, "Love and do what you will," expressing that true love—self-giving, sacrificial, and unconditional—aligns all our actions with God's will. In loving one another as Jesus loved, we become credible witnesses of the Gospel. Pope Benedict XVI emphasized that "only through service to others can God open our eyes to what He does for us and to how much He loves us." When we love as Jesus loves, our lives radiate the love of God, drawing others to Him.

The vision in Revelation speaks of a new heaven and a new earth, a place where "God will dwell with them" and "there shall be no more death or mourning, wailing or pain" (Revelation 21:3-4). This vision reminds us that God's promise is not only of personal salvation but the transformation of all creation. God's "making all things new" is a work that begins here and now, as we live out our Christian calling. Saint Teresa of Ávila captured this idea beautifully when she said, "Christ has no body now on earth but yours, no hands but yours, no feet but yours." In the presence of Christ, we bring about the renewal of creation. Pope Francis, in Laudato Si', teaches that our care for one another and creation is part of our role in God's redemptive plan. When we love with Christ's love, our actions participate in this "new creation," where divisions are healed, and God's peace reigns.

The reading from Acts shows Paul and Barnabas returning to the communities they had established, strengthening their faith and encouraging them with the words, "Through many hardships we must enter the kingdom of God" (Acts 14:22). This realistic view of discipleship acknowledges the challenges of following Christ but also the joy of sharing in His redemptive work. The 20th-century theologian Hans Urs von Balthasar wrote about the Christian call to participate in Christ's suffering for the sake of love, reminding us that "love alone is credible." Discipleship is demanding, but these challenges are part of our purification, drawing us closer to Christ and forming us in His image. Pope Saint John Paul II, who knew suffering personally, once said, "Do not be afraid to welcome Christ and accept His power." It is through our willingness to bear hardship for love of God and neighbor that the Kingdom takes root in our lives. Living the Command to Love and Renew the World These readings challenge us to live out a love that is sacrificial, redemptive, and deeply transformative. Jesus's command to "love one another as I have loved you" calls us to be His hands and feet, to bear witness to His love in a way that renews and builds up His kingdom. As Teilhard de Chardin, another 20th-century theologian, wrote, "The day will come when, after harnessing space, the winds, the tides, and gravitation, we shall harness for God the energies of love, and on that day, for the second time in the history of the world, we shall have discovered fire." In this Eucharist, let us ask God to kindle that fire within us. May we embrace the commandment to love and participate in His work of making all things new. And as we encounter challenges, may we draw strength from knowing that Christ walks with us, transforming our trials into means of grace and pathways to His Kingdom

Sixth Sunday of Easter

The Church is very wise in the planning of the liturgical calendar. It seems like we are always in preparation for the next big thing in the cycle. The liturgical year begins with the season of Advent, a time of preparation for the coming of Christ. However, even in Advent, this holy time can be viewed as a kind of two-part season. The Christmas season, although among the shortest liturgical seasons, takes us in about two weeks from the infant Christ to the Christ beginning His earthly ministry following His Baptism. We then go for a short period of time into the season of Ordinary Time, this post-Epiphany season, in which we are fully immersed in the ministry of Christ. The great and holy season of Lent, the time of penance and preparation before the yearly commemoration of the Easter mysteries can be seen as logically flowing from this time of Christ's earthly ministry and can even be seen to be in two parts, in a similar way to Advent. The time of remote preparation for Easter can be seen from Ash Wednesday and the first three-and-a-half weeks of Lent (in which the Lord Jesus gives us all those rich parables basically on prayer, fasting, almsgiving, and forgiveness) to around the end of fourth week of Lent, when we begin to engage in our Gospel with the confrontations which led Our Lord to suffer His Passion, Death, and Resurrection.

Following the time of the Sacred Triduum (which, truth be told, is its own liturgical season, clearly differentiated from Lent), we have the Easter season, which is, outside of Ordinary Time, the longest of the seasons. However, we can view even this Easter season, one in which we bathe in the light of His Risen Glory, Christ Our Lord, as a season of preparation. We can view all of the liturgical season of Easter as a remote and proximate preparation for the coming of the Holy Spirit in Pentecost. (And, if I may be candid, I find it a real shame that we do not have a season of Pentecost in the liturgical calendar; imagine how nice it would be to have around two weeks of red vestments at the start of Ordinary Time.)

Beginning this week, we begin the proximate preparations for the coming of the Holy Spirit in Pentecost. It is said that, in many ways, the Holy Spirit is the forgotten Person of the Most Blessed Trinity. Perhaps this is because, in many ways, He is the most intangible.

Make no mistake, though – the Holy Spirit is God. He is the Lord, the giver of life, as we profess each Sunday and solemnity in the Nicene Creed. But how do we experience the Holy Spirit? The sure and certain guide is *The Catechism of the Catholic Church*.

In the Catechism (688), we read the following:

The Church, a communion living in the faith of the apostles which she transmits, is the place where we know the Holy Spirit:

- in the Scriptures He inspired;
- in the Tradition, to which the Church Fathers are always timely witnesses;
- in the Church's Magisterium, which he assists;
- in the sacramental liturgy, through its words and symbols, in which the Holy Spirit puts us into communion with Christ;
- in prayer, wherein he intercedes for us;
- in the charisms and ministries by which the Church is built up;
- in the signs of apostolic and missionary life;

- in the witness of saints through whom he manifests his holiness and continues the work of salvation.

First, we can find the Holy Spirit in the Deposit of Divine Revelation, meaning we can see the hand of the Holy Spirit guiding the Bible and the Sacred Tradition of the Church. Do we recognize that the Sacred Scripture's true author is ultimately God? Yes, God works through the divinely inspired authors, so that correctly conceived, accurately expressed, and truthfully composed, the Bible in its Canon, but never forget that God is the author of the Bible.

In our preparation for Pentecost, we might read with open hearts and minds the book that we have been reading throughout the entire Easter season – the Acts of the Apostles. In many ways, this book is the sequel to the Gospel of Luke and it shares the same author. Read Acts and look for the stories of where that Third Person of the Trinity is the protagonist.

Second, we can find the Holy Spirit in the Sacred Liturgy. When you attend Mass, look for the number of times that the Holy Spirit is invoked, especially during the Eucharistic Prayer.

Third, we find the Holy Spirit in the lives of the saints. Learn about the saints, blessed, venerables, and the servants of God and look to where the Holy Spirit was clearly guiding them throughout their lives. Some figures whom you might want to examine include Saint John Henry Newman, Venerable Mother Catherine McAuley, the Foundress of the Religious Sisters of Mercy, and the Servant of God, Romano Guardini, the great 20th Century spiritual writer.

The Holy Spirit is coming soon in Pentecost, but He is actively present, powerfully showering us with His seven-fold gifts. Use this remaining time in the Easter season to prepare for the Holy Spirit!

Ascension

What Jesus had to tell the Apostles that they could not bear at that moment was the experience of the Paschal Mystery- the Passion, Death, Resurrection, Ascension, and Pentecost. If the Lord had told his Apostles everything that was going to happen in the Upper Room, they would not have grasped it. They might have been confused, perhaps even scandalized. They had to wait, to go through the events of this sacred time of Easter, to experience the joy and the fear, the lows and the highs of the entire paschal mystery, so that they could understand, through the eyes of faith, these central events in the life of Christ.

Perhaps at times you, like me, can be impatient. Not just impatient with others or with ourselves, but even with the Lord. What's going to happen next? What's at the root of this impatience in our lives? I think that, at its essence, it's fear and a lack of trust. Fear that the Lord is not reigning triumphantly in our world and that by his resurrection and ascension, he has not truly conquered this fallen world. Lacking in the trust in the plan for the Lord in our lives, we look to ourselves or to others to provide that security and to be that safety net. And, as the Lord says: "It cannot be that way with you.'

Only when we see everything in our lives in and through the complete Paschal Mystery, not segmenting it, placing the Passion in one box, the Resurrection in another, the Ascension in yet another and so on, will our lives make sense. Ultimately, it is the gift of the Spirit, he who will lead us to all truth, he who is coming at Pentecost, who will grant us the grace to bear what it is we cannot hear and understand right now. As Christ ascends in glory to his Father and Our Father, may we have the security and consolation of knowing that things are, ultimately, going to be ok, and will go, ultimately, according to God's plan for our lives.

Seventh Sunday of Easter

In today's Gospel, Jesus prays, "that they may all be one, as you, Father, are in me and I in you, that they also may be in us" (John 17:21). This prayer for unity is foundational for the Church's understanding of ecumenism, the pursuit of Christian unity. But what does true ecumenism look like for us as Catholics? Guided by the teachings of Vatican II, papal texts, and the United States Conference of Catholic Bishops (USCCB), let's explore what it means to live this call to unity authentically and in fidelity to Christ.

In John 17, Jesus's prayer for unity comes from His intimate relationship with the Father. This unity is not superficial or based on mere human agreement; it is grounded in the divine love shared between the Father and the Son. Jesus invites us to share in this love, and through it, to build unity with one another. The Second Vatican Council captured this when it wrote in *Unitatis Redintegratio*, the Decree on Ecumenism, that ecumenism is "inspired by the Holy Spirit," and that "Christ summons the Church to this pursuit" (UR, 1). True ecumenism is not a project of compromise but a divine call to share in the unity of the Trinity itself.

Vatican II emphasized that the work of ecumenism requires both truth and charity. The Council fathers wrote, "There can be no ecumenism worthy of the name without interior conversion," calling all Catholics to personal holiness and openness to the Spirit (UR, 7). True ecumenism starts with our hearts, with a conversion that allows us to seek unity, not for our purposes, but for the sake of Christ's mission.

Pope John Paul II, in his encyclical *Ut Unum Sint* ("That They May Be One"), reaffirmed this commitment to unity in truth, saying, "Dialogue is not simply an exchange of ideas. In some way, it is always an 'exchange of gifts'" (Ut Unum Sint, 28). In true ecumenism, we respect other Christian traditions, recognizing where the Spirit is at work in them, while also remaining grounded in the fullness of truth that the Catholic Church preserves.

The US Conference of Catholic Bishops highlights the importance of the laity in ecumenism. In its document *Called to be Catholic*, the bishops emphasize that every Catholic has a role in promoting unity, primarily through our witness of love. When we live out the love of Christ in our everyday lives—when we respect and love our Protestant and Orthodox brothers and sisters—we build bridges that go beyond theological debate. The USCCB encourages parishes to engage in local ecumenical efforts, such as shared prayer services, charitable works, and community outreach, as a way to foster mutual understanding and respect.

True ecumenism also recognizes the reality that we are not yet fully united, particularly in our understanding of the Eucharist. The *Directory for the Application of Principles and Norms on Ecumenism*, issued by the Pontifical Council for Promoting Christian Unity, reminds us that while we long to share fully in the Eucharist, this sacrament is a "sign of unity already attained" and "a source of the grace that brings unity to completion." We respect this sacred difference, but we still long and work for the day when all Christians can come to the table as one.

Pope Benedict XVI, in *Sacramentum Caritatis*, called the Eucharist the "sacrament of charity" and a powerful prayer for unity. He reminded Catholics that when we participate in the Eucharist, we also pray for all Christians to be united in "one body, one Spirit" (Eph 4:4). So, even though we experience pain at our incomplete unity, every Mass becomes a plea for the healing of divisions and the fulfillment of Jesus's prayer.

How can we live out this call to unity today? First, by fostering respect and understanding in our conversations with other Christians. When we encounter those from other denominations, let us do so with charity, recognizing the common baptism we share and the work of the Spirit among them. The USCCB encourages us to enter into "spiritual ecumenism"—praying together, whenever appropriate, for unity and understanding.

In our own prayer lives, let us keep ecumenism in our hearts. Pray for the healing of divisions, for the guidance of the Holy Spirit, and for the humility to pursue unity, not as a victory but as a gift from God. Saint Pope John XXIII, who initiated Vatican II, prayed daily for unity, saying, "In essentials, unity; in non-essentials, liberty; in all things, charity."

As we reflect on Jesus's prayer "that they may all be one," let us ask for the grace to pursue true ecumenism, rooted in fidelity to the truth, openness to dialogue, and love for one another. Let us answer Christ's call to unity in all our actions, knowing that our efforts for unity will ultimately be completed by God, who makes "all things new" (Rev 21:5).

Today, may we pray and work for the day when all Christians will stand together, as one family in faith, sharing in the fullness of Christ's love and truth.

Pentecost

Let's look at the recent history of our Church: On a chilly winter day, Jan. 25, 1959, Angelo Roncalli, guiding the Barque of Peter known as John XXIII, stood at the Basilica of Saint Paul Outside the Walls, gathered members of the Roman Curia, and called for a Second Vatican Ecumenical Council. The Church historians, Giuseppe Alberigo and Joseph Komonchak, describe the reactions of most as "stunned silence." And, on Oct. 11, 1962, the first session of Vatican II began, a work which John XXIII did not live to see completed, but one that has profoundly influenced not only the Catholic Church, both Western and Eastern, but the Orthodox Church, most of the Protestant ecclesial communions, and indeed, the course of history. This is an act of the Holy Spirit.

On July 25, 1968, John's successor, Giovanni Battista Montini, steering the Barque of Peter known as Paul VI, released an encyclical that proved to be prescient, "Humanae Vitae." Paul consulted and consulted, asked and took advice, and then decided that condoning as an acceptable act the use of artificial birth control would be an act that would cheapen human life and would lead to an abortive mentality. He was right. New York State legalized abortion in 1970 and, in 1973, the scourge of abortion was released in the whole United States of America. Paul's decision to follow the consistent magisterium of the Church, the fonts of Divine Revelation - Sacred Scripture and Sacred Tradition - as well as natural law, was a brave act. And it was an act of the Holy Spirit.

On Oct. 16, 1978, the cardinals elected Karol Wojtyla, the first non-Italian pope in centuries. This vigorous younger man, only 58 at the time, stood in the central balcony of Saint Peter's Basilica and uttered the words: "Do not be afraid." It was his influence, his steadfastness, his insight that guided the Church and the world away from the horrors of Communism and began the New Evangelization. His pontificate as John Paul II was an act of the Holy Spirit.

On Feb. 11, 2013, Joseph Ratzinger, navigating the ship that is the Church as Benedict XVI, at a private consistory of cardinals gathered to approve canonizations and beatifications of some saints, at the very end of the meeting, announced for the first time in centuries, that a pope would resign and that he would retire and spend his remaining years in study and prayer. His catechesis, his writings, his gentle presence, and, yes, even his resignation was an act of the Holy Spirit.

Now we have Jorge Mario Cardinal Bergoglio as our Holy Father, Pope Francis. Elected on March 13, 2013, Francis has brought the Church and the faith into the public eye in a new, exciting, and, yes, challenging way. He has, in his years to date, reintroduced to the forefront of our minds concepts that the Mother Church had never really forgotten - mercy, accompaniment, option for the poor and Gospel joy - to a world that often has forgotten. His election and his papacy is an ongoing act of the Spirit.

It is the Holy Spirit of God, that bond of love and knowledge that exists from all eternity between God the Father and God the Son, that is active and present in the Church and the world. This Spirit is so much more than just the natural progress and decline that exists in the course of history, as is thought of in the work of some modern philosophers. No, the Holy Spirit is a Divine Person. The Holy Spirit is love and knowledge and it is the same Holy Spirit that guides the Church throughout all the ages.

Do we believe this? Do we trust in this saving truth? Yes, there are problems and difficulties, fears and anxieties that perplex the Church today. To list them would extend this already long homily. We know the threat of a secularized culture against our faith; we are aware of the many challenges to the reality that is natural law that come from attacks against a traditional understanding of marriage, family and gender. Sadly, we know the stories of the modern martyrs, our brothers and sisters whose blood is shed out of hatred of the faith. We know that to the world, the Church can appear divided at times on issues like divorce and remarriage without benefit of declaration of the invalidity of marriage and other issues of pastoral practice. And yet, in all of this, the Spirit is the principal operating agent.

On May 8, 2017, in a homily given at his daily Mass in the chapel of the Domus Santa Marta, His Holiness, Pope Francis said: "The Spirit is the gift of God, of this God, our Father who always surprises us. The God of surprises ... Why? Because He is a living God, who dwells in us, a God who moves our hearts, a God who is in the Church and walks with us and in this journey He surprises us. It is He who has the creativity to create the world, the creativity to create new things every day. He is the God who surprises us."

This is a call to trust. The Holy Spirit, God, is in charge of the Church and the world, not us. It is our task to discern with the Church the movement of the Holy Spirit so that we can see his action in the world. Pray about this concept on this Pentecost Sunday, that the Holy Spirit of God, so that Third Person of the Most Blessed Trinity, will flood our minds and lead them to insight that we can bask in the sure and certain knowledge that He is in charge of steering this ship, not us, and He alone will guide us into our true port, Heaven.

Trinity Sunday

Karl Rahner, the 20th century Jesuit theologian, in his book, *The Trinity* (1970), opined that, for the average Catholic, one could dispense with the entire doctrine of the Blessed Trinity and few would notice in their daily life. This statement has always bothered me tremendously, but in many ways, for the average Catholic, and not only the laity, the doctrine of the Most Blessed Trinity, although certainly acknowledged, does not play an explicit part in their daily life. This is true even for us priests and deacons, especially when we are called to preach on Trinity Sunday. How many times have we heard the homilist simply proclaim this as a mystery, something that we must accept as a tenant of the faith, yet no real attempt is made to engage this most essential element of our faith, namely who God is in himself!

Today' celebration of Trinity Sunday reminds of the truth of the matter. We as human beings are called to communion. We need communion with each other because the God in whose image and likeness we are created is, in Himself, a communion of love and knowledge. In the Most Blessed Trinity, we see how we are called to live and to love as Christians in the world. Pope Emeritus Benedict XVI in a Sunday Angelus in 2009 said:

> Three Persons who are *one God* because the Father is love, the Son is love, the Spirit is love. God is wholly and only love, the purest, infinite and eternal love. He does not live in splendid solitude but rather is an inexhaustible source of life that is ceaselessly given and communicated. To a certain

extent we can perceive this by observing both the macro-universe: our earth, the planets, the stars, the galaxies; and the micro-universe: cells, atoms, elementary particles. The "name" of the Blessed Trinity is, in a certain sense, imprinted upon all things because all that exists, down to the last particle, is in relation; in this way we catch a glimpse of God as relationship and ultimately, Creator Love. All things derive from love, aspire to love and move impelled by love, though naturally with varying degrees of awareness and freedom. "... The strongest proof that we are made in the image of the Trinity is this: love alone makes us happy because we live in a relationship, and we live to love and to be loved. Borrowing an analogy from biology, we could say that imprinted upon his "genome", the human being bears a profound mark of the Trinity, of God as Love.

We as human beings, in our very nature, mirror that inner life of the Triune God and in no greater way is that expressed than when we strive to live lives of communion with one another. Listen to the words from Saint Paul to the Corinthians. The Apostle Paul (2nd Corinthians 13:11-13) exhorts us to love one another, to greet each other with a holy kiss, in other words, to live a life of harmony. And how does he end this passage? With nothing less than the words offered as the first option for the greeting in the introductory rites of the Mass: "The grace of our Lord Jesus Christ and the love of God and the fellowship of the Holy Spirit be with all of you."

The inner life of God in the Most Blessed Trinity offers to us the model of how we are to live as Christians, namely in the world, yet not of the world, yes, but also not apart from one another. We all called to be leaven in the world, to transform the world, by our presence and by the daily living of the Gospel. The answer to how to live as an authentic Christian in the world today is found when we as Christians can live our lives in communion with our brothers and sisters in the world.

One of the more interesting films of the past 20 years or so, Tom Hanks' *Castaway* (2000, directed by Robert Zemeckis), was the story of a man, Chuck Nolan, whose Federal Express freight airplane crashes on a desert island. This modern-day Robinson Crusoe is trapped, stranded on this island, which is somewhere, I think, between where Gilligan was and where the cast of "Lost" had been.

Thanks be to God, Hanks' character, Chuck, was on an airplane that was carrying almost everything one could need to survive. And survive he does, learning how to cook, clean, build a shelter, even in one particularly harrowing scene, do minor dental surgery. He has everything that one could need to survive except for company.

In one of the more interesting parts of this movie, there is complete silence, no dialogue. Chuck is just trying to survive. Yet he is longing for someone to dialogue with. He needs companionship. So, if there is no one to talk to, what can one do? Well, in the case of this character, he meets Wilson. Wilson functions as the "Man Friday" to Chuck's Caruso, with one telling exception. Wilson is a volleyball! Granted, Wilson is a volleyball with a bloody handprint for his face. And the character played by Hanks forms a relationship with Wilson. They even have arguments, at least in the lead character's head, leading to one of the more heartbreaking scenes in this movie — while on a raft at sea during an attempt to escape, Wilson floats away. When Chuck notices this, it is too late, leaving him to shout, "Wilson, come back, I'm sorry!" Why do I mention this film in a homily on Trinity Sunday? For one reason — we can have all of the basic necessities of life and still not have what we need to be fully human. We need community!

Why do we as human beings need community? Because Almighty God in Himself is a Communion of Three Persons, yet One Godhead. You might say that being in communion with others is built into who we are as human beings, created by God in his image and likeness. We are called to communion, because God is a Communion!

Corpus Christi

Saint Thomas Aquinas, towards the end of his life, was asked to write a treatise, a compendium, on Eucharistic theology, to encapsulate all that we as Catholics believe about the Eucharist. He wrote and he wrote and he wrote, until he could write no more, and in a rare moment of frustration, he took the manuscript that he was writing and threw it at the foot of the crucifix. The story is that the corpus, the figure of Christ on the Cross, came to life and spoke to St. Thomas Aquinas. Jesus spoke to Thomas and said: "Thomas Aquinas, no one has written as well as you have concerning my Eucharistic body and blood. Whatever it is that you want the most, I will grant you." Imagine if Jesus spoke to you, right here, right now, and said to you, "Whatever it is you want most in the world, I will grant to you." What would you say? What would I say? What would I really say? Thomas Aquinas looked at the Lord squarely in the eyes and said three little words, and, of course, they were in Latin, because that's what they were speaking then, three little words: *NIL NISI TE*, which means NOTHING BUT YOU. What do you want most in the world? Nothing but you.

Thomas Aquinas knew that if he has Jesus in the Eucharist, he has everything. Padre Pio once said: "It would be easier for the world to survive without the sun, than to do without Holy Mass." The Eucharist is the single most important thing in the universe, the most precious gift that God has given to man. It is not just a sign, not just a symbol. It is Christ, true God, true man, sacramentally present to us in the form of bread and wine that is, after consecration, truly, substantially changed into Christ's body and blood. The Eucharist is not just a "nice thing," not merely a symbolic sign of sharing and community, it is Christ's true Body and true Blood.

At Holy Mass, we come to celebrate the single greatest gift- God, the Second Person of the Most Blessed Trinity, the Son of God, comes to us, to feed, to strengthen, to nourish us in the simplest of accidents, the simplest of food, the staple of the diet of the Palestinian culture of Jesus' day, and indeed, even within this Italian culture in which we find ourselves, bread and wine. He who created the stars of the universe, who fashioned the heavens, who singlehandedly harrowed the halls of hell, freeing all of humanity from the snares of Satan by his death and resurrection, he comes to us in this simple, humble way. Jesus, ever meek and humble of heart, the Sacred Heart whom we honor and adore, this Jesus comes to us as food; he enters us, becomes one with us, and, unlike earthly food which becomes integrated into us, this heavenly food makes us becomes more and more like him whom we receive.

I have to say that I love Mass. I really truly do. It's the main reason I'm a priest. When I was a high school student, every single day we had to attend Mass as part of the school day, and I thank God that we did. I would look up at the altar and see those priests who were teaching me in classes, reverently celebrating Mass, and I wanted to do that, too. I wanted to be like them, because they had this great gift, this great ability. I have been so blessed as in my life as a priest because every single day in my life (except for one, actually the day Pope Benedict XVI came to Yankee Stadium in New York and we were not permitted to concelebrate, only to distribute Holy Communion), I have been able, and sometimes, due to pastoral circumstances several times a day, offer Holy Mass. I know how unworthy I am to do this; I know I am sinner, but I know that this is why I was born. In spite of me, through my hands and the hands of my brother priests, at this altar, heaven and earth meet, time and eternity kiss, God and man are once again reconciled. What we do here at this altar is nothing less than the unbloodied sacrifice of Calvary. What we celebrate at this altar is the nothing less than the entire paschal mystery. And you and I get to receive him, Jesus, our Lord.

In the tabernacle, the Living God dwells; when we reverently receive his Body and Blood in the Eucharist, we too become tabernacles, too, living, walking, breathing tabernacles, shrines in the flesh of the Living God.

Two things, then, for us: first if we believe in the Real Presence of Christ, how do we receive the Eucharistic Lord? Do we consciously show reverence and acknowledgment to the Real Presence of Christ in the Eucharist or has it become a mere casual act? And further, does the reverence we show draw more attentive to ourselves or to the Eucharist Lord? Do we prepare ourselves for Mass, acknowledging consciously what it is we are doing and where we are, in spite of the distractions, even the ones that can come due to our state of lives? The distractions that a young parent will have will be different than that of a priest, and they are things and people that must be attended, even right before Mass, but perhaps we can take a moment before Mass and quickly say the prayer of Jean-Jacques Olier, the founder of the Sulpicians: "O Jesus, living in Mary, come and live in your servants, in the spirit of holiness, in the fullness of your power, in the perfection of your ways, in the truth of your virtues, in the communion of your mysteries. Rule over every adverse power, in your Spirit, for the glory of the Father. Amen."

Second, what are the moral implications of our receptions of Holy Communion? How is our day different because we have received Holy Communion? Is my day different because I have celebrated Mass? Do I recognize the Christ who lives in you and transforms you more and more by the Communion that you had received? Do we strive to see Christ in each other and then to be Christ to each other, recognizing that everyone whom we meet, especially the people that God has placed in our daily lives, whom we see every single day and whom we sometimes don't appreciate as much as we should? Today, on this feast of Corpus Christi, filled with love incarnate, the Eucharistic Jesus, shine like the sun, and let everyone whom you encounter know, by your love, that they, too, are shining like the sun, too.

The Solemnity of the Most Sacred Heart of Jesus

Today, we celebrate the Solemnity of the Sacred Heart of Jesus, a feast that invites us to contemplate the profound and infinite love of Christ for humanity. This love is not distant or abstract; it is deeply personal and intimate, symbolized by the Sacred Heart. Through Scripture, theology, and devotion, we are reminded that the Sacred Heart is the very source of mercy, compassion, and redemption.

The readings today draw us into this mystery. In Ezekiel, God is portrayed as the shepherd who searches for His lost sheep. In Romans, Paul assures us of the boundless love poured into our hearts through the Holy Spirit. Finally, in the Gospel, Jesus speaks of the Good Shepherd who rejoices over one lost sheep. These passages illuminate the heart of Christ, which beats with an unrelenting love for each of us.

The devotion to the Sacred Heart has been deeply enriched by the Church's Magisterium. Pope Pius XII, in his encyclical *Haurietis Aquas* (*You Shall Draw Waters*), describes the Sacred Heart as the "symbol and image of the infinite love of Christ." He writes that the devotion to the Sacred Heart is not merely sentimental but profoundly theological, rooted in the reality of the Incarnation and the Passion.

Pope Francis has emphasized the Sacred Heart as a model for tenderness and mercy, calling us to reflect on how Jesus' heart reaches out to the marginalized, the wounded, and the lost. He reminds us that the heart of Christ is "an open door" through which we experience God's mercy and are invited to extend it to others.

Devotion to the Sacred Heart is accompanied by the Twelve Promises revealed to Saint Margaret Mary Alacoque. Among these promises, we are assured of Christ's peace, consolation, and mercy. They are as follows:

1. I will give them all the graces necessary for their state of life.
2. I will give peace in their families.
3. I will console them in all their troubles.
4. I will be their refuge in life and especially in death.
5. I will abundantly bless all their undertakings.
6. Sinners shall find in my Heart the source and infinite ocean of mercy.
7. Tepid souls shall become fervent.
8. Fervent souls shall rise speedily to great perfection.
9. I will bless those places wherein the image of My Sacred Heart shall be exposed and venerated.
10. I will give to priests the power to touch the most hardened hearts.
11. Persons who propagate this devotion shall have their names eternally written in my Heart.
12. In the excess of the mercy of my Heart, I promise you that my all powerful love will grant to all those who will receive Communion on the First Fridays, for nine consecutive months, the grace of final repentance: they will not die in my displeasure, nor without receiving the sacraments; and my Heart will be their secure refuge in that last hour.

Perhaps most strikingly, He promises: *"Sinners will find in My Heart the source and infinite ocean of mercy."*

This aligns perfectly with today's Gospel, where the Good Shepherd leaves the ninety-nine to search for the one lost sheep. The Sacred Heart of Jesus does not give up on anyone. Instead, it seeks, heals, and rejoices when even one soul is brought back to God.

Saint Thomas Aquinas offers profound insight into the love of Christ, particularly in his reflections on the Passion. He teaches that Christ's heart is both a symbol and a reality of His love, which is demonstrated most fully in His willingness to suffer and die for us. Aquinas writes:

> *"The Passion of Christ is sufficient to serve as an example for the entire life of a Christian. Whoever wishes to live perfectly should do nothing but disdain what Christ disdained on the cross, and desire what He desired, for the cross exemplifies every virtue."*

The pierced heart of Christ, which flowed with blood and water, becomes a fountain of sacramental life and grace. For Aquinas, this outpouring of love is not only salvific but also a model for how we are called to love: selflessly, sacrificially, and with great mercy.

The Jesuits have played a significant role in promoting devotion to the Sacred Heart, particularly through the work of Saint Claude de la Colombière, who was a spiritual director to Saint Margaret Mary. Jesuit spirituality emphasizes the Sacred Heart as the center of Jesus' mission, calling us to a deep, interior love that translates into action. Jesuit theologians often link the Sacred Heart to the Eucharist. In the Eucharist, we encounter the same love symbolized by the Sacred Heart—a love that nourishes, heals, and strengthens us to be Christ's hands and heart in the world. Saint Ignatius of Loyola's prayer, *"Take, Lord, and receive,"* can be seen as a response to the love offered by the Sacred Heart: giving ourselves entirely to the one who gave Himself completely for us.

In Ezekiel, God promises to seek out His sheep, rescue them from danger, and tend to their wounds. This is a foreshadowing of Christ, the Good Shepherd, whose heart burns with love for the lost and broken. In Romans, Paul reminds us that Christ's love is most clearly demonstrated in His death for sinners. This is the love of the Sacred Heart—a love that goes to the cross to bring us back to God.

The Gospel parable of the lost sheep invites us to see ourselves as both the sheep and the shepherd. As the sheep, we experience Christ's merciful love that seeks us out when we are lost. As the shepherd, we are called to embody that same love for others, reaching out with compassion and mercy.

Devotion to the Sacred Heart is not limited to private prayer or liturgical celebration. It must shape how we live. The Sacred Heart calls us to be merciful by Imitating Christ's mercy in our relationships and extending forgiveness generously; to seek the lost by reaching out to those who are marginalized, wounded, or spiritually adrift; and to bear witness by living a life that reflects the self-giving love of Christ, especially in acts of service and sacrifice.

The Catechism of the Catholic Church reminds us: *"By His death and Resurrection, Jesus Christ has 'opened' heaven to us. The life of the Blessed Trinity consists of perfect love."* (1026) The Sacred Heart reveals that perfect love and invites us into it.

As we reflect on the Sacred Heart of Jesus, let us be drawn to the depths of His love—a love that seeks us when we are lost, sustains us in our struggles, and calls us to share that love with the world.

Inspired by the promises of the Sacred Heart, the teaching of the Church, and the wisdom of saints and theologians, may we respond to Christ's love with hearts that are humble, merciful, and aflame with charity. Let us pray with Saint Claude de la Colombière: *"O Sacred Heart of Jesus, teach me to love You with my whole heart and to share Your love with all whom I meet."*

The Solemnity of Saints Peter and Paul

Today, we celebrate two giants of the Church, Saints Peter and Paul, who embody the complementary yet distinct dimensions of the Church's mission. Their lives and martyrdom stand as a testament to faith, humility, and boldness in proclaiming Christ. As we reflect on the readings for this solemnity, we see how Peter and Paul's unique roles mirror the multifaceted mission of the Church.

In today's Gospel (John 21:15–19), we hear Christ's triple question to Peter: "Do you love me?" Each response from Peter is met with a commission: "Feed my lambs...Tend my sheep." This is Peter's reinstatement after his threefold denial during the Passion and his elevation as the chief shepherd of the Church. In this moment, Peter assumes his role as the visible foundation of unity. As the Catechism reminds us: *"Simon Peter holds the first place in the college of the Twelve; Jesus entrusted a unique mission to him. Through a revelation from the Father, Peter had confessed: 'You are the Christ, the Son of the living God.' Our Lord then declared to him: 'You are Peter, and on this rock I will build my Church'"* (CCC 552).

Peter's authority as the first pope highlights the *Petrine mode* of the Church, described by Hans Urs von Balthasar. This mode emphasizes the Church's institutional and hierarchical dimension, ensuring unity and fidelity to Christ's teaching. It is a gift of divine grace, not merely human governance.

In the second reading (Galatians 1:11–20), Paul recounts his dramatic conversion and call to proclaim the Gospel to the Gentiles. His life exemplifies the Church's *charismatic mode*, another dimension identified by Balthasar. This mode underscores the Spirit's dynamic and creative work, breaking boundaries and expanding the Church's mission.

Paul's encounter with Christ transformed him into an apostle of grace, preaching the radical message that salvation comes through faith in Jesus Christ, not adherence to the law. Vatican II's *Dei Verbum* echoes this understanding: *"The apostles handed on to their successors what they themselves had received from Christ's lips, from living with Him, and from what He did, or that they had learned through the prompting of the Holy Spirit"* (*Dei Verbum*, 7). Paul's writings and missionary zeal show us that the Church is called not only to preserve but to proclaim and expand the Gospel in every age and culture.

The first reading (Acts 3:1–10) recounts Peter's miraculous healing of the lame man at the Temple gate. His words, "In the name of Jesus Christ of Nazareth, rise and walk," reveal the *sacramental mode* of the Church. The Church is not merely an institution or a movement but the very Body of Christ, through which grace is mediated. Saint Thomas Aquinas explains the power of Christ's name: *"The name of Jesus is efficacious because it signifies the whole of Christ's salvific work, the fullness of grace and truth made present among us."*

Through Peter and Paul, we see how the Church brings Christ's healing and redemptive power to the world. Vatican II's *Lumen Gentium* reminds us: *"The Church, in Christ, is a sacrament—a sign and instrument of communion with God and of unity among all people"* (*Lumen Gentium*, 1).

The Solemnity of Saints Peter and Paul reminds us that the Church is both universal and particular, hierarchical and charismatic, sacramental and missionary. These dimensions are not in conflict but in harmony, as modeled by the lives of these two apostles. Their martyrdom in Rome unites them forever as the pillars of the Church.

Pope Benedict XVI reflected on this complementarity, saying: *"Peter and Paul, though very different in character and mission, both served one Church, the one Church of Christ. They teach us the meaning of unity in diversity."* Pope Francis continues this theme, emphasizing the importance of mission: *"The Church is called to reach all people, to bring them the joy of the Gospel, showing that faith is not a burden but a source of liberation and life."* (*Evangelii Gaudium*, 21).

As we honor Saints Peter and Paul, we are called to live out the faith they handed down. Like Peter, we must remain rooted in the Church's teachings, standing firm on the rock of Christ. Like Paul, we must be bold in bringing the Gospel to the margins, sharing the message of grace and freedom in Christ.

In the words of Saint Thomas Aquinas, let us remember: *"Faith is the first step toward eternal life, but charity perfects it, leading us to the vision of God."* May the prayers of Saints Peter and Paul strengthen us as we strive to build a Church that reflects the fullness of Christ's mission: faithful, dynamic, and alive with the Spirit.

The Assumption of the Blessed Virgin Mary

Mary, our Mother, is our guide in everything. Her life, both on earth and in heaven, offers us a pattern to follow. She is the Immaculate Conception, free from the stain of Original Sin, a gift that prepared her to be the Mother of God and the first and most perfect disciple of Christ. Saint Thomas Aquinas reflects on Mary's immaculate state, writing: *"The Blessed Virgin, because she is the Mother of God, has a certain infinite dignity from the infinite good, which is God."*(*Summa Theologiae*, III, q. 27, a. 1).

As the Immaculate Conception, Mary lived her life in perfect conformity to the will of God. Her faith, humility, and obedience shine as virtues that we, who bear the burden of Original Sin, are called to imitate. She teaches us to trust in God's promises, as she did in her *fiat*: "Behold, I am the handmaid of the Lord; let it be to me according to your word" (Luke 1:38).

Today, on the solemnity of the Assumption, we celebrate Mary being taken up, body and soul, into heavenly glory. This is a foretaste of what is promised to all the faithful. Pope Pius XII, in his apostolic constitution *Munificentissimus Deus*, proclaimed the dogma of the Assumption, declaring: *"The Immaculate Virgin, preserved free from all stain of original sin, was taken up body and soul into heavenly glory, and exalted by the Lord as Queen over all things."*

Mary's Assumption is the logical consequence of her Immaculate Conception. Saint John Paul II reflected that: *"The Assumption of the Blessed Virgin is a singular participation in her Son's Resurrection and an anticipation of the resurrection of other Christians"* (*General Audience*, July 2, 1997).

Unlike Mary, our bodies decay after death, but the Assumption points to our ultimate hope. As *The Catechism of the Catholic Church* teaches: "At the end of time, the Kingdom of God will come in its fullness. Then the just will reign with Christ forever, glorified in body and soul, and the material universe itself will be transformed" (1060). Mary's Assumption gives us hope that we, too, may share in this glorification, provided we follow her example and live as true disciples of Christ.

In the Eucharist, we are given the Bread of Heaven, the very Body and Blood of Christ, to strengthen us on our journey. Saint Thomas Aquinas reminds us: *"The Eucharist is the Sacrament of Love; it signifies Love, it produces Love. The Eucharist is the consummation of the whole spiritual life."*

Mary, as the first tabernacle of Christ, points us to the Eucharist as the source and summit of our faith. By receiving the Eucharist, we are united with Christ and given the grace to follow Mary's example of holiness. In her Assumption, Mary is crowned as Queen of Heaven and Earth. Pope Francis has described her queenship as rooted in service: *"As Mother and Queen, she exercises her reign by serving her children, helping us in our needs with her maternal love. She watches over us in our journey and sustains our hope."* (*Regina Caeli Address*, May 13, 2013).

As Queen, Mary intercedes for us, helping us to remain faithful and hopeful as we strive to live lives of holiness. Saint Bernard of Clairvaux beautifully assures us of her role as our advocate: *"In dangers, in doubts, in difficulties, think of Mary, call upon Mary. Let her name be ever on your lips. Following her, you shall not go astray."*

Today is a day of hope and promise. Mary's Assumption reminds us that God's ultimate plan for humanity is not decay and death, but life and glory. Mary, who was preserved from sin and assumed into heaven, leads the way for us. Her life and destiny foreshadow the reality that awaits the faithful.

Let us strive to follow her example by living lives of faith, humility, and obedience. Let us draw strength from the Eucharist and cling to the hope of eternal life. And as we honor Mary, let us make her prayer our own: *"My soul magnifies the Lord, and my spirit rejoices in God my Savior"* (Luke 1:46-47).

With hearts full of gratitude and hope, let us commend ourselves to Mary, the Queen of Heaven and Earth, trusting that through her intercession, we will one day share in the glory of her Son, Jesus Christ.

The Solemnity of All Saints

This great solemnity is one in which we recall to our memory the company of the Saints, the Holy Ones of God. This Holy Day reminds us of us of what should be our two main goals in our life: what should be our ultimate destination, Heaven, and how we can get there, by centering our life around the Lord, by becoming saints.

What does the Lord really want from us? Perhaps only this- to make the Lord and the Lord alone the center of our life. He is asking us more than anything to refocus our spiritual eyesight, to move from our spiritual myopia and readjust our vision to focus on what truly matters, namely the Lord and the things of the Lord.

The Church is more than just her living members. There is the great Communion of Saints who spur us onwards. Who are the saints? Bishop Robert Barron writes:

> The saints, in a word, are those who have allowed Jesus to get into their boats and who have thereby become, not super-human or angelic, but fully human, as alive as God intended them to be. The entire purpose of the church, as we saw, is to produce saints. Scripture, tradition, liturgy, official teaching, moral instruction, and the sacraments are all means to the end of fostering friendship with God.[1]

The saint is one who, simply put, has God and God alone as his or her center of ultimate concern. Bishop Barron further writes:

---

[1] *Catholicism*, 196-197.

The holiness of God is like a white light: pure, simple, complete. But when that lights shines, as it were, through the prism of individual human lives, it breaks into an infinite variety of colors. The four women we've considered in this chapter couldn't be more different from one another—and that is why each one allows a unique dimension of the divine holiness to appear. God's grace shone through the particularity of Edith Stein and gave us the clarity of her intellectual work and the beauty of her martyrdom; it shone through the uniqueness of Therese of Lisieux and gave us the little way; it shone through the individuality of Katharine Drexel and it produced a miracle of transfigured justice; it shone through the unrepeatable identity of Mother Teresa and brought forth the Missionaries of Charity. The church revels in the variety of its saints because it needs such diversity in order to represent, with even relative adequacy, the infinite intensity of God's goodness.[2]

Let's aim to make it home, back to our origin and source, the center of our ultimate concern, Christ Jesus the Lord! Let's aim to become who we were created to be, namely saints, those who have God and the things of God as our area of ultimate concern!

---

[2] *Catholicism*, 223.

The Commemoration of All Souls

I think that All Souls Day can teach us two lessons: one, to understand and to embrace our own mortality and two, the Christian obligation to pray for the dead.

First, there is the very real need for *Memento mori*- remember that we are all passing away. The Capuchin Crypt near Piazza Barberini in Rome teaches us this lesson, as does the Capela dos Ossas in Portugal, whose inscription over the chapel's door reads: "We bones that here are, for yours await." I have seen the grave in which one day I will be placed in Brooklyn's Greenwood Cemetery. Every day, we come a little bit closer to it. It's a reminder to me that I am slowly decaying, getting older, and that, with each day, I am approaching death. And so too is everyone in my life whom I love. And I hate the thought of it. It's scary.

As I get older, it seems that the days just run into each other, that the pace is so much quicker, and time spent with family and close friends get shorter and shorter. Now, this is all part of being an adult, but it can be a disconcerting feeling.

The truth is, with each day I am passing away and so is everyone else, just like everyone before us. But the even greater truth is that death is not the end. It is not, as Shakespeare calls it, the "unknown country," but something we know by faith, something that we grasp, as the Apostle Paul tells us, "hoping against hope." We have a place prepared for us who believe and who try, even in our own imperfect way, in heaven.

This feast of All Souls is a beautiful one, one which makes us stop and take account of where we are and where we are going. These are our mysteries of our own dying and rising in Christ. Through faith and through our incorporation into the Body of Christ by baptism, we have the assurance that all those whom we have loved and lost, all those whom we love and cherish here on earth, we will, please God, be united around the heavenly throne one day.

Two resolutions, then, in light of this fact of our faith: first, let us live each day on this earth as if it is our last, cherishing in and relishing in the gift of our lives in this plane of reality. The people with whom we are blessed are far too precious to neglect. And second, we should not neglect those who have gone before us; we need to pray for them, the poor souls in purgatory, for where they are, we will be, hoping for the eternal light to be shown to us.

All of this is passing. But what really matters in the end, the three things, faith, hope, and the greatest of these, love, well, that's' what lasts.

Second Sunday in Ordinary Time

In today's Gospel, we hear the words of Jesus at the wedding in Cana, responding to His mother's quiet prompting: "Woman, what does this have to do with me? My hour has not yet come." (John 2:4). These words might strike us as puzzling or even dismissive, but they carry a profound significance. This phrase—"my hour"—echoes throughout the Gospel of John and points to Jesus' mission and the purpose for which He came into the world. To understand it is to begin to understand the very heart of Jesus' life, death, and resurrection.

At the wedding in Cana, Jesus is with His mother and His disciples when they run out of wine—a potentially humiliating situation for the bridegroom and his family. Mary, noticing this, simply brings the need to her Son, saying, "They have no wine." Though His response may seem unexpected, Jesus isn't rejecting His mother's concern. Instead, He is drawing attention to a divine timing that extends beyond this present moment.

The "hour" to which Jesus refers is the hour of His Passion, the moment of His ultimate sacrifice on the Cross. This "hour" will be the climax of His mission: the giving of His life for the salvation of the world. By saying, "My hour has not yet come," Jesus is indicating that the fullness of His mission has yet to unfold. He knows that each sign and each miracle He performs will lead Him closer to that decisive moment of His crucifixion and resurrection. Every action He takes is guided by a greater plan, by the will of His Father.

Yet even here, in this moment, Jesus performs His first public miracle. Moved by His mother's faith and trust in Him, He transforms water into wine, revealing His glory and deepening the faith of His disciples. This miracle at Cana foreshadows the ultimate transformation that will occur at the Last Supper, when He takes wine and declares it to be His Blood, poured out for the forgiveness of sins. Jesus' "hour" will indeed come, and when it does, He will give us the gift of His very self, turning the ordinary elements of bread and wine into His Body and Blood to nourish and redeem us.

What does this mean for us today? In a world that often expects instant answers and quick solutions, Jesus' words remind us that God's timing is different from our own. There are moments in our lives when we, like Mary, bring our needs, worries, or requests to Jesus, hoping for an immediate answer or resolution. We may feel like Mary, saying, "They have no wine"—whether that means the wine of peace in a struggling relationship, the wine of healing in the face of illness, or the wine of hope when facing despair. Yet Jesus may respond with a mysterious silence or a reminder that His hour, His time, is not ours.

To live as followers of Christ is to trust that God's timing, though it may seem hidden or delayed, is always perfect. Jesus knew that every moment of His ministry was ordered toward the fulfillment of His Father's plan. He teaches us to surrender our own plans, hopes, and desires to the Father's timing, even when we do not fully understand it. Mary shows us this surrender as well. After Jesus' response, she does not argue or insist; instead, she turns to the servants and simply says, "Do whatever He tells you." Mary's faith is a model for us. She trusts that Jesus will act, even if she does not know how or when.

This Gospel invites us to imitate both Mary's faith and Jesus' obedience to the Father's will. In our own lives, we often face situations where we feel we are waiting for God's "hour" to come, waiting for the answer to our prayers. But we are invited, even in that waiting, to trust and to act with faith, just as the servants did in filling the jars with water, believing that Jesus will transform our lives in His time.

Today, let us bring our needs, our emptiness, and our thirst to Jesus, trusting that He sees and hears us. And let us remember that even when His answer is "not yet," He is leading us toward a greater purpose, a deeper joy, and a more profound union with Him. His hour will come, and when it does, it will bring us more than we could ever ask for or imagine.

May we, like Mary, have the courage to say, "Do whatever He tells you," and may we trust in the perfect timing of the One who loves us beyond measure

.

Third Sunday in Ordinary Time

Today's Gospel presents us with two powerful moments in the life of Jesus. First, we hear Luke's opening words, setting the scene for a Gospel that is "an orderly account" to reveal the life and mission of Jesus. Then, we enter a synagogue in Nazareth, where Jesus takes up the scroll of Isaiah and declares that the ancient words of prophecy are being fulfilled in that very moment: "Today this scripture has been fulfilled in your hearing" (Luke 4:21).

Hans Urs von Balthasar, one of the most profound Catholic theologians of the 20th century, offers a unique perspective on this Gospel passage. Balthasar often emphasizes the idea of God's self-revelation in Christ as a divine drama, a story in which God enters human history to enact His love. In this light, today's reading can be seen as a climactic moment in that divine drama. Jesus is not merely reading words; He is embodying and fulfilling them. He is the living Word of God, making Himself known, not as an abstract idea or distant deity, but as one who is radically present to His people—here and now.

Imagine the scene. Jesus, freshly baptized and filled with the Spirit, enters His hometown synagogue, stands up to read, and deliberately chooses the passage from Isaiah that speaks of the Messiah who will bring "good news to the poor... release to the captives... sight to the blind... and freedom to the oppressed" (Isaiah 61:1-2). With this declaration, He does not simply proclaim a mission; He proclaims Himself as the fulfillment of that mission. According to Balthasar, this is Jesus stepping fully into the drama of salvation as both God and man, revealing the fullness of His identity and purpose.

Balthasar would remind us that in Jesus, God doesn't just announce freedom from a distance. He steps into our captivity, our blindness, our oppression, and makes them His own. He shares in our struggles and bears our burdens, and in doing so, transforms them from within. This is a God who enters the depths of our human condition—not only to bring comfort but to offer a new creation, a new beginning.

But notice the word that Jesus emphasizes: *today.* "Today this scripture has been fulfilled in your hearing." Balthasar understood that the concept of "today" is central to the Gospel. Jesus is the eternal Word made flesh, and He brings eternity into each present moment. Through Him, the "today" of salvation is made accessible to every human heart, at every moment in history. Jesus' proclamation in the synagogue is not merely an event in the past; it is a living Word that continues to resound in our lives. Jesus is saying to us, here and now: *Today, I come to free you. Today, I come to heal you. Today, I come to transform your life.*

What does this mean for us? It means that every moment of our lives is an opportunity for encounter with Christ. No situation, no hardship, no moment of despair is beyond the reach of God's redeeming presence. Jesus' proclamation in Nazareth is an invitation for us to open our lives to Him, to allow His Word to enter our struggles and transform them.

But there's a further challenge: just as Jesus embodied the Word He proclaimed, we are called to embody the Gospel in our lives. This is what Balthasar refers to as the "theo-drama" – the idea that God invites each of us to play a role in the divine drama of salvation. We are not mere spectators; we are called to be participants, to take up the mantle of Christ's mission to bring good news to the poor, freedom to the captive, and sight to the blind.

The fulfillment of Jesus' mission is ongoing, and we are called to be a part of it. In a world that often feels fragmented, divided, and spiritually blind, we are asked to carry Christ's presence into our daily lives. We are called to be "good news" to those around us, especially to those who suffer or are forgotten. We may feel unworthy, hesitant, or ill-equipped for this task, but Jesus assures us: "The Spirit of the Lord is upon me." Just as the Spirit was upon Jesus, so too does the Spirit rest upon us, empowering us to live this mission in our own unique ways.

Balthasar often wrote about the need for Christians to surrender to God's love, allowing it to shape us into vessels of His grace. This surrender is our "yes" to God's invitation to enter the divine drama. When we open ourselves to the presence of Christ and say "yes" to His call, our lives become a continuation of the Gospel. Each act of kindness, each moment of forgiveness, each gesture of compassion becomes a living "today" of God's love in the world.

As we reflect on this Gospel, let us remember that the promise of Isaiah is fulfilled not only in Jesus but through Jesus in us. Today, as we listen to His words, may we let them enter our hearts, transform our lives, and move us to act. May we, in our own small ways, bring sight to the blind, comfort to the brokenhearted, and freedom to those in chains. And may we trust that, as we do so, the Spirit of the Lord is truly upon us, working through us to make His love known in the world.

Fourth Sunday in Ordinary Time

It's interesting that the central action connecting the first reading, taken from the Old Testament Book of Nehemiah, and the New Testament's Gospel of Luke involves something that we take for granted, something so common that we don't necessarily even pay attention to it: reading! What a gift the written word is. What a gift the ability to read is. And what a gift it is to read aloud to others, particularly to proclaim the Word of God when gathered as a community.

We encounter the priest, Ezra, in today's first reading, gathering together all of the people of Jerusalem old enough to comprehend what exactly was occurring, and he reads to them. "The whole people gathered as one...called upon Ezra the scribe to bring forth the book of the law of Moses which the Lord had commanded for Israel." (Nehemiah 8:1) Ezra read aloud the words of sacred Scripture and "all the people, their hands raised high, answered, 'Amen, amen!' Then they bowed down and prostrated themselves before the Lord." (Nehemiah 8:6)

Recall the impact of this action of gathering the people together in one place and reading aloud to them. No doubt only a few people in the gathered crowd could read but this public proclamation means something so much more — reading aloud gathers the people of God, who are inspired by the Spirit, to reflection, and, ultimately, mission.

In the Gospel, we read that, filled with the Spirit, the Lord Jesus enters the Synagogue in the town where he was raised and reads aloud, and even more so than just plain reading, proclaims the

Scriptures. He who is the Word of God made flesh proclaims the word to God's people, gathered together for worship and prayer.

What then can we glean from these proclamations, first from Ezra the priest and then from Jesus, the one, true, high priest of the new and eternal covenant? I think a number of things: first, on a practical level, and at the risk of sounding like a public service announcement, reading is fundamental!

The printed page has whole other worlds on it waiting to be explored. We do not read as much as we should. We live in an age of instant information. We are a very quick-paced, very visual culture now, one, not to propagate a stereotype, that likes to get its information in under 130 characters. These novels and poems that I am recommending are certainly more than 130 characters. They require, for the most part, an investment of self and a commitment of energy and interest that many sadly are not either eager, willing, or able to spend in our culture, due to time constraints, as well as the reality of having never been introduced to the joys of reading in general.

Second, reading the Word of God has power. The responsorial psalm tells us "Your words, Lord, are spirit and life." God communicates his life to us in so many ways, most especially in the grace of the Sacraments, and, in particular, in the Eucharist, his Real Presence. But God also communicates to us in and through the inspired Word of God, found in sacred Scripture. All too often parishioners tell their priests that the Liturgy of the Word is something just to be endured. The lectors are not prepared, the psalm is sloppily sung (or mumbled through, if recited), and the priest and deacon, joyless, proclaim the Gospel, and, to top it all off, give a functional homily at best! The proclamation of God's word is key — to paraphrase the

Ethiopian Eunuch and the Apostle Philip from the Acts of the Apostles, how can we know the Lord unless someone tells us about him? The primary way we learn about the Lord as Catholics is at Mass, so the effective proclamation of the Word of God is essential for us.

Reading is a gift! And to proclaim God's holy Word given to us in sacred Scripture is a tremendous gift. And, hearing the Word proclaimed wisely and well by lectors, deacons, and priests can change lives! When we read at Mass, may our response and the response of the people to whom we minister be what Ezra the priest encountered: "all the people, their hands raised high, answered, 'Amen, amen!' Then they bowed down and prostrated themselves before the Lord" (Nehemiah 8:6), not for us but at the mighty power of God revealed in the Bible!

Fifth Sunday in Ordinary Time

In today's reading from 1 Corinthians 15, Saint Paul reminds the Corinthians of the Gospel he proclaimed, the same Gospel he *received*. This is a profound declaration: the Gospel is not something Paul invented, but a treasure handed down to him and entrusted to others.

This passage offers us a window into the heart of what we call Sacred Tradition, one of the two fonts of Divine Revelation, along with Sacred Scripture. Tradition is not simply the repetition of old customs; it is the living transmission of God's Word, given to the apostles and passed down through the Church, under the guidance of the Holy Spirit.

The Second Vatican Council's document *Dei Verbum* (The Word of God) beautifully articulates the relationship between Scripture and Tradition. It teaches: *"Sacred tradition and Sacred Scripture make up a single sacred deposit of the Word of God, which is entrusted to the Church." (Dei Verbum, 10).*

Tradition and Scripture are inseparable because they both flow from the same divine source. Scripture is the written Word of God, while Tradition preserves and transmits the fullness of the faith that Christ entrusted to the apostles. Together, they nourish and guide the Church, ensuring that the Gospel remains alive and effective in every age.

The Catechism echoes *Dei Verbum* and highlights how Tradition operates: *"Through Tradition, the Church, in her doctrine, life, and worship, perpetuates and transmits to every generation all that she herself is, all that she believes."* (CCC 78) This dynamic, living

Tradition is not static or outdated. It grows and deepens through prayer, study, and the lived experience of the faithful. Yet it always remains faithful to the original deposit of faith. Saint Paul's words—*"I handed on to you what I also received"*—are an invitation to recognize that we are recipients of a treasure, not innovators of it.

Pope Benedict XVI often spoke of Tradition as a *living encounter with Christ*. He taught: *"Tradition is not a collection of things or words, like a box of dead things. Tradition is the river of new life that flows from the origins, from Christ down to us, and makes us participate in God's history with humanity."*

For Benedict, Tradition is dynamic—it connects us to Christ through the Church and allows the Holy Spirit to continually renew us. This perspective reminds us that Tradition is not about preserving the past for its own sake; it is about living the faith here and now, in continuity with the apostles and the saints.

Pope Francis emphasizes that Tradition is inherently missionary. He says: *"Tradition is the guarantee of the future, it is the root from which we take the sap that makes the tree grow... [It] is like the roots of the tree, which give life so that the tree grows, flowers, and bears fruit."*

Tradition equips us to bring the Gospel to the modern world. It is not a museum piece, but a source of strength and vitality, enabling the Church to respond to new challenges while remaining faithful to her mission. Just as Paul handed on the Gospel to the Corinthians, so are we called to share the faith in ways that resonate with our time, always grounded in the truth.

Saint Thomas Aquinas sheds light on the theological foundation of Tradition. He explains that the Word of God is received through both Scripture and Tradition because human reason alone cannot grasp the fullness of divine truth. He writes: *"The teaching of the Church is derived from divine revelation, which is communicated in a way fitting to human understanding through Scripture and the apostolic preaching."* (*Summa Theologiae*, I-II, Q.1, Art.10).

Aquinas also underscores the communal nature of Tradition. It is not merely individual interpretation but the collective wisdom of the Church, guided by the Holy Spirit. This is why Tradition is safeguarded by the Magisterium, ensuring that it remains faithful to Christ's teaching and does not stray into error.

Tradition is most vividly expressed in the lives of the saints. Consider the great saints who handed on the faith in their time, such as Saint Augustine, Saint Francis of Assisi, or Saint Teresa of Avila. Their lives were steeped in Scripture and Tradition, yet they found ways to present the faith anew to their contemporaries. Their witness shows us how Tradition is both faithful and creative. It is faithful because it preserves the unchanging truth of the Gospel; it is creative because it finds new ways to communicate that truth in the language of every age.

Saint Paul's words to the Corinthians challenge us to ask: How are we handing on what we have received? Tradition is not something we simply inherit; it is something we are called to participate in. Every time we teach the faith to our children, live out the Gospel in our daily lives, or bring Christ's love to others, we are participating in the living Tradition of the Church.

In a world that often values innovation over fidelity, the Church's Tradition reminds us of the timeless truths that anchor us. Yet it also calls us to be creative and missionary, finding new ways to proclaim the Gospel to a world in need.

As we reflect on today's reading, let us give thanks for the gift of Tradition, through which we encounter Christ and share in the richness of the faith. Let us commit to preserving and sharing this treasure, remembering the words of Pope Francis: *"Tradition is the root from which we take the sap that makes the tree grow."*

May the Holy Spirit guide us in living and handing on the faith, so that, like Saint Paul, we may one day say with confidence: *"I handed on to you as of first importance what I also received."*

Sixth Sunday in Ordinary Time

Today, the sacred liturgy presents us with a profound tapestry woven from the words of the prophet Jeremiah, the psalmist, Saint Paul, and the Gospel according to Saint Luke. Each thread speaks of a singular truth: the beatitude of trusting in God.

Jeremiah paints a stark contrast: "Cursed is the one who trusts in human beings... Blessed is the one who trusts in the Lord." This is not a condemnation of human relationships or achievements but a prophetic warning against idolatry of the self and the ephemeral. Trusting solely in human strength dries up the soul, like a barren bush in the desert.

The Catechism of the Catholic Church (CCC 301) reminds us that God sustains every being in existence; to sever our hearts from Him is to disconnect from the very source of life. Saint Thomas Aquinas, in his Summa Theologiae (II-II, q. 129), teaches that fortitude—rooted in trust in God—is the virtue that strengthens us against the fear of earthly loss.

The psalm echoes Jeremiah: the blessed one is "like a tree planted by streams of water," flourishing because it draws from an unending source. This image reflects the life of grace, the indwelling of the Holy Spirit (CCC 1997), nourishing us through prayer, the sacraments, and the Word of God.

Pope Francis, in Evangelii Gaudium (n. 7), reminds us that "the joy of the Gospel fills the hearts and lives of all who encounter Jesus." The blessed man delights in the law of the Lord because he has encountered not a set of rules, but the living God.

Saint Paul confronts the denial of the resurrection: "If Christ has not been raised, your faith is vain." The resurrection is not an abstract doctrine but the very heart of our hope (CCC 655). Without it, our lives are unmoored, subject to despair. Aquinas affirms that the resurrection is the cause of our justification (III, q. 53, a. 1), for in rising, Christ conquered sin and death, opening the way to eternal life.

In Luke's Gospel, Jesus speaks directly to the crowd, proclaiming blessings and woes. "Blessed are you who are poor... woe to you who are rich." This reversal shocks us because it subverts worldly expectations. Yet, these beatitudes are not a mere call to material poverty but an invitation to spiritual poverty—humility that acknowledges our total dependence on God (CCC 2546).

Pope Francis often speaks of this radical Gospel. In Laudato Si' (n. 222), he says, "Christian spirituality proposes an alternative understanding of the quality of life, and encourages a prophetic and contemplative lifestyle, one capable of deep enjoyment free of the obsession with consumption."

The Scriptures today call us to examine: Where is our trust? In fleeting pleasures or in the eternal God? Are we trees planted by living waters or withering shrubs in the desert? Let us anchor our lives in Christ, the Risen Lord, drawing strength from the sacraments, delighting in His Word, and living the paradoxical joy of the Beatitudes. In this, we find the blessedness that the world cannot give, and death cannot take away.

Seventh Sunday in Ordinary Time

Sermon on the Plain

"Be merciful, just as your Father is merciful." (Luke 6:36)

In Luke's *Sermon on the Plain* (Luke 6:27–38), Jesus presents a radical teaching that challenges every natural instinct. He commands His followers to love their enemies, bless those who curse them, and give without expecting anything in return. At the heart of this teaching is the command: *"Be merciful, just as your Father is merciful."*

Mercy is the key to understanding this passage. It is the foundation of God's relationship with humanity and the essence of how we are called to live as His children. But what does it mean to be merciful, and how can we live this out in a world often characterized by conflict, self-interest, and division?

Saint Thomas Aquinas offers profound insights into the nature of mercy, helping us to see it not only as a human virtue but as a reflection of the very nature of God.

Aquinas defines mercy, or *misericordia*, as a "heartfelt sorrow" for another's suffering, accompanied by a desire to alleviate it. In the *Summa Theologiae*, he explains that mercy arises from charity—the love that wills the good of another. It is not a passive feeling but a virtue that moves us to action. Mercy, Aquinas teaches, is grounded in our shared humanity; we are moved to compassion because we see our own vulnerability in the suffering of others.

He writes: *"Of all the virtues which relate to our neighbor, mercy is the greatest, for it belongs to mercy to be bountiful to others, and, what is more, to succor their needs."* (ST II-II, Q.30, Art. 4). For Aquinas, mercy is not optional; it is essential to living out the Gospel, because it reflects the mercy of God Himself.

Aquinas also emphasizes that mercy is central to God's nature. While God is perfectly just, His mercy does not contradict His justice. Rather, mercy is *"the most excellent work of His power"* (ST I, Q.21, Art. 3). It is through mercy that God reveals His infinite goodness, forgiving sins and offering grace to those who do not deserve it.

This divine mercy is not weakness but strength. It is the power to restore, to heal, and to bring hope. Aquinas argues that God's mercy is a model for human mercy. As creatures made in His image, we are called to imitate this divine mercy, not only in our actions but in our very disposition toward others.

In the *Sermon on the Plain*, Jesus shows us what mercy looks like in action, namely loving enemies, rather than retaliating against them; blessing those who curse us and praying for those who mistreat us; and giving generously without expecting repayment. Each of these commands overturns the logic of the world, which often operates on retribution and self-interest. Instead, Jesus calls us to a higher standard: to act with the same mercy that God shows to us.

Mercy, as Aquinas reminds us, begins with seeing the suffering of others. It involves recognizing their pain and allowing it to move our hearts. But it does not stop there; it compels us to respond. When we forgive, when we give, when we choose love over hatred, we participate in God's work of mercy in the world.

Living out this mercy is not easy. It requires us to let go of pride, selfishness, and the desire for vengeance. Yet, Jesus assures us that mercy is its own reward. In Luke 6:38, He says: *"Give, and it will be given to you. A good measure, packed together, shaken down, and overflowing, will be poured into your lap. For the measure with which you measure will in return be measured out to you."*

Mercy opens us to the abundance of God's grace. When we show mercy to others, we draw closer to the heart of God and experience His mercy more deeply in our own lives.

The transformative power of mercy is beautifully depicted in the story of *Les Misérables*. Jean Valjean, a hardened convict, is transformed by the mercy of the bishop who forgives him and gives him another chance. That act of mercy not only changes Valjean's life but becomes the foundation for a life dedicated to compassion and justice.

In our own lives, we are called to be like that bishop, extending mercy to those who least deserve it. This could mean forgiving a family member who has hurt us, helping someone in need without expecting anything in return, or choosing to see the humanity in someone society has cast aside.

To be merciful, as our Father is merciful, is both a challenge and a gift. It requires us to go beyond the limits of our natural inclinations and to love as God loves. Saint Thomas Aquinas reminds us that mercy is not merely an act of charity but a reflection of divine justice and perfection. It is a way of participating in the very life of God.

As we meditate on Jesus' words in the *Sermon on the Plain*, let us pray for the grace to live out this call to mercy. May we see the suffering of others with the eyes of compassion, respond with the heart of charity, and act with the strength of divine love. In doing so, we will not only transform the lives of others but become more fully who God created us to be: instruments of His mercy in the world.

Eighth Sunday in Ordinary Time

Today's readings reveal how words and actions reveal what lies within us. In Sirach, we hear that "when a sieve is shaken, the husks appear." It's a reminder that when we are "shaken," our true inner life shows itself, and in this unveiling, our words are powerful indicators. Jesus takes it a step further in today's Gospel: "For from the fullness of the heart the mouth speaks."

Today's readings, which highlight how words and actions reflect the depths of our hearts, can also be understood through the lens of beauty—both as Hans Urs von Balthasar and Saint Thomas Aquinas describe it. Their teachings reveal that beauty is not just something to be admired but a profound way to encounter God and communicate His love to the world.

Hans Urs von Balthasar, one of the most influential Catholic theologians of the 20th century, emphasized that beauty is a transcendental—one of the fundamental qualities of being, alongside truth and goodness. For Balthasar, beauty is not a mere aesthetic experience but a window into the divine. He believed that beauty draws us out of ourselves, lifting us toward God.

Hans Urs von Balthasar often emphasized that what we say and do manifests our relationship with God. Just as in art or film, where directors use visuals to convey deeper truths, Balthasar argued that our lives should communicate God's beauty. We are, in a way, "directing" the film of our lives. If our hearts are filled with love and grace, we become a work of divine art—a testament to God's love that can inspire others.

In his monumental work *The Glory of the Lord*, Balthasar writes: *"Beauty is the disinterested, yet compelling, presence of the divine splendor in creation."* When we encounter true beauty—whether in nature, art, or a life well-lived—it reveals God's glory and stirs a longing in us for something greater. This beauty is not superficial; it comes from harmony, integrity, and radiance, which point to the Creator.

Balthasar extends this understanding of beauty to our lives as Christians. He argued that our words and actions should radiate God's beauty, serving as an evangelizing force. Just as a beautiful painting captivates its viewer, a life filled with grace and love attracts others to Christ. When Jesus says, *"For from the fullness of the heart the mouth speaks"* (Luke 6:45), He challenges us to ensure that the "artwork" of our lives reflects the divine beauty within.

Saint Thomas Aquinas provides a framework for understanding beauty that complements Balthasar's vision. For Aquinas, beauty has three essential qualities: first, Integrity (Wholeness) – Something is beautiful when it is complete, lacking nothing necessary; second, Proportion (Harmony) – Beauty is found in the harmonious arrangement of parts, creating balance and order; and finally, Clarity (Radiance) – Beauty shines forth, revealing its truth and purpose.

Aquinas teaches that God is the ultimate source of beauty because He embodies perfect integrity, harmony, and radiance. He writes: *"The beautiful is that which pleases when seen"* (ST I-II, Q.27, Art.1). This pleasure is not merely sensory but spiritual—it is a recognition of God's perfection reflected in creation.

In human life, Aquinas explains, beauty is most fully realized when our actions align with God's will. When we live virtuously, our lives take on a "radiance" that points others to God. This is why mercy, charity, and humility are not only good but beautiful—they reflect the harmony of a soul in communion with God.

When we bring together the insights of Balthasar and Aquinas, we see that beauty is not just something we observe but something we are called to embody. Just as an artist carefully crafts each detail of a painting, so must we shape our lives through our choices, striving for integrity, harmony, and radiance in our relationship with God and others. Our actions must echo Aquinas' teaching that true beauty is rooted in charity, and they must fulfill Balthasar's call to let one's life radiate the splendor of God.

Similarly, in our everyday lives, the small acts of kindness, forgiveness, and mercy we offer to others can reveal the beauty of God's love. Whether it's comforting a friend in need, speaking words of encouragement, or standing up for justice, these actions are brushstrokes in the masterpiece God calls us to create. Possible ways for us to progress in this might be to first examine our integrity: Are our words and actions consistent with our faith? Second, to strive to live with wholeness and authenticity, so that your life reflects God's integrity; seek harmony. In our relationships and responsibilities, ask where there may be discord or imbalance; and third, bring harmony by acting with patience, humility, and love; and finally, and perhaps most importantly, to let your faith radiate: Like a light shining on a hill, let your faith and charity be evident in how you treat others. Be a source of hope and inspiration.

In today's readings, we are reminded that our words and actions reveal the state of our hearts. Saint Thomas Aquinas and Hans Urs von Balthasar challenge us to go further, recognizing that our lives are meant to radiate the beauty of God. To live this way is to embody the Gospel, making our lives a work of art that points others to the divine Artist.

Let us pray for the grace to live with integrity, harmony, and clarity, so that through us, God's beauty may shine forth. May our words and deeds proclaim, as Sirach says, the "fullness of the heart," and may that fullness always be filled with the love of Christ

Ninth Sunday in Ordinary Time

Today, as we reflect on Paul's words in Galatians 1:1-2, 6-10, we enter into his passionate defense of the Gospel against distortions and false teachings. Paul confronts the Galatians with a question that speaks to their deepest priorities and allegiances: *What are we living for, and whom do we serve?* His urgency speaks to his unwavering commitment to Christ and his refusal to dilute the truth, even at the cost of popularity. This passage invites us to consider the virtues essential for steadfastness in the Gospel—a theme that Saint Thomas Aquinas sheds light on through his teachings on the virtues.

Aquinas defined virtues as "good habits of the soul," characteristics that help us act in alignment with our true purpose and, ultimately, draw closer to God. For Aquinas, virtues are more than moral skills; they are gifts that help us respond to God's grace and live in harmony with the truth. This Gospel truth is what Paul is defending: a truth that frees us and calls us to courage, integrity, and authentic love. Aquinas identified four cardinal virtues that provide a foundation for our lives as Christians: prudence, justice, fortitude, and temperance.

Aquinas calls prudence the "charioteer" of virtues, as it guides all other virtues and directs them toward the good. In this letter, Paul urges the Galatians to discern the true Gospel from distortions, exercising a prudence that sees beyond human approval to seek God's will. In our lives, prudence encourages us to pause, reflect, and make choices aligned with the truth of Christ, even when pressured to conform.

This virtue, according to Aquinas, is about giving others what they are due. For Paul, justice means honoring the truth of the Gospel itself. His frustration with the Galatians comes from his desire for them to uphold justice by giving God the trust and fidelity due to Him. Practicing justice in our faith means staying true to what we have received from Christ and the Church, even when it requires self-sacrifice.

Fortitude: Paul's example of fortitude is striking here. He is bold, unafraid of losing followers or favor, if it means defending the Gospel. Aquinas calls fortitude the courage to endure difficulties for the sake of the good, even in the face of hardship. True fortitude helps us stand firm in our faith and convictions, not out of pride, but because we know that God's truth is worth every trial.

Finally, temperance regulates our desires, helping us seek God above all else. Paul's dismay at the Galatians' quick turn to other teachings is a call to temperance. Aquinas teaches that temperance allows us to control our impulses and focus on lasting, eternal good rather than being swayed by temporary allurements. In our faith journey, temperance keeps us grounded, helping us resist the temptations that might pull us away from the Gospel.

Saint Thomas also identifies three theological virtues—faith, hope, and charity—as direct gifts from God, nourishing our relationship with Him. These virtues anchor Paul's message. His faith in Christ fuels his boldness, his hope keeps him steadfast, and his charity impels him to lovingly correct the Galatians.

Through these virtues, Aquinas encourages us to live the truth of the Gospel in a way that is both humble and unwavering. Today, may we renew our commitment to cultivate these virtues in our lives, letting them guide us to live in a manner worthy of the Gospel of Christ, even when the world pulls us in another direction. In this way, we not only honor Paul's words to the Galatians but also bear witness to the beauty of a life rooted in truth and love.

Tenth Sunday in Ordinary Time

The Letter to the Galatians is one of Saint Paul's most fervent and urgent writings, addressing a significant crisis in the early Church. The Galatian Christians, primarily Gentile converts, were being influenced by a group known as the "Judaizers." These individuals taught that salvation required adherence to Jewish laws, especially circumcision, in addition to faith in Christ.

Paul's response is a theological and emotional tour de force. He defends the Gospel he proclaimed as a message of grace, not law; of freedom, not bondage. For Paul, the insistence on circumcision symbolized a rejection of the sufficiency of Christ's sacrifice and a regression into the "yoke of slavery."

This letter was not just a corrective for the Galatians but a manifesto for the entire Christian faith. Its themes of liberty, identity, and the transformative power of grace resonate across centuries, speaking to anyone tempted to reduce the Gospel to mere rules or human effort.

Galatians 5:1 serves as a cornerstone of Paul's message: "For freedom Christ has set us free." Freedom, in the biblical sense, is not a license to do whatever we please. Rather, it is the liberation from sin and the law's inability to justify, enabling us to live fully in God's grace.

For the Galatians, the "yoke of slavery" referred to the Mosaic law, which could not bring about salvation but only point to humanity's need for Christ. For us, the yoke can take many forms: reliance on self-righteousness, the pursuit of worldly success, or even the endless striving for perfection. Paul's message is clear: we are free in Christ, not because of what we do, but because of what He has done.

Saint Thomas Aquinas illuminates Paul's teachings by distinguishing between the "old law" and the "new law." The old law, Aquinas explains, was given to prepare humanity for the coming of Christ. It revealed sin but could not heal it. The new law, rooted in grace, accomplishes what the old law could not: it transforms the heart.

Aquinas underscores that the new law is not primarily about external observance but about the internal movement of the Holy Spirit. Justification comes not from adherence to rituals but from *fides caritate formata*—faith formed by charity. This faith is dynamic, engaging the believer in a living relationship with Christ that bears fruit in love and good works.

In Galatians 5:1, Aquinas sees an invitation to embrace the freedom of the Spirit. This freedom does not abolish the moral law but fulfills it. When we live in grace, our actions flow from love rather than fear, and we are no longer enslaved by the need to earn our salvation. For Aquinas, this is the perfection of human life: to be united with God in love.

Paul's call to "stand fast" in freedom challenges us to reflect on our own spiritual lives. Do we live as people liberated by grace, or do we allow ourselves to be burdened by self-reliance, perfectionism, or the fear of failure?

The freedom Paul describes is not a rejection of moral responsibility but a reorientation of the heart. When we live in grace, we obey God not out of obligation but out of love. This is the freedom that enables us to serve others joyfully, confident in the knowledge that we are already justified in Christ.

The Letter to the Galatians reminds us that the Gospel is a message of liberation. Saint Thomas Aquinas helps us see that this freedom is not an abstract concept but the lived reality of grace transforming our hearts, showing us the power of transformation and the joy of living in freedom.

May we, like Paul, stand firm in the freedom Christ has won for us. Let us reject the yoke of slavery in whatever form it takes, living as people freed by grace to love and serve. For in Christ Jesus, it is not what we do, but who we are in Him that counts.

Eleventh Sunday in Ordinary Time

"Then Nathan said to David, 'You are the man!'" (2 Samuel 12:7)

The passage from 2 Samuel 12 brings us to a dramatic moment in the life of King David. David, the man after God's own heart, has fallen grievously. His sin began with lust for Bathsheba, leading to adultery and culminating in the murder of her husband, Uriah the Hittite.

For a time, David thought his sins were hidden. But God, through the prophet Nathan, brings them into the light. Nathan's parable of the rich man stealing the poor man's lamb pierces David's conscience, and the words, *"You are the man!"* cut to the core. David's response is humble and immediate: *"I have sinned against the Lord"* (v. 13).

David's story is not just about sin; it is about the mercy of God and the transformative power of repentance. This episode invites us to confront our own failings, not in despair, but in hope, trusting in God's forgiveness and the call to a renewed life.

David's journey from sin to repentance mirrors the call to conversion in every Christian life. Conversion, or *metanoia*, is not a one-time event but an ongoing process. It is the daily turning of the heart toward God, recognizing our sins, and striving to live in His grace.

In David's case, his recognition of sin came through the voice of a prophet. For us, it often comes through the voice of our conscience, illuminated by the Word of God, the sacraments, and the teachings of the Church. Conversion requires courage to face the truth about ourselves, humility to admit our faults, and faith to seek God's mercy.

David's prayer in Psalm 51, composed after this episode, gives voice to the heart of true repentance: *"Create in me a clean heart, O God, and renew a right spirit within me. Cast me not away from your presence, and take not your Holy Spirit from me"* (Psalm 51:10-11). This is the posture of every penitent soul: a plea not for what we deserve but for God's grace to make us new.

Saint Thomas Aquinas offers profound insight into the nature of sin, grace, and conversion. In his *Summa Theologiae*, Aquinas teaches that sin is a turning away from God, the ultimate good, and a disordered turning toward created things. David's sin, like all sin, was rooted in this disordered love—seeking personal pleasure and power at the expense of fidelity to God and justice toward others.

Yet Aquinas also emphasizes the boundless mercy of God. He writes that God's grace is always sufficient to draw the sinner back to Himself, provided the sinner is willing to cooperate with it. In David's case, his willingness to acknowledge his sin and repent allowed God's grace to transform his heart.

Aquinas identifies contrition as the first step in conversion. True contrition, he explains, is not merely fear of punishment but sorrow for having offended God, who is infinitely good. This sorrow moves the will to seek forgiveness, opening the soul to the healing power of grace. David's confession, *"I have sinned against the Lord,"* reflects this deep contrition.

Finally, Aquinas reminds us that God's mercy does not negate justice. While David is forgiven, he still faces the consequences of his actions. This balance of mercy and justice is a reminder that sin has real effects, yet God's grace can bring good even from our failures.

No one is beyond the reach of God's mercy. Like David, we are all called to confront our sins, seek forgiveness, and allow God's grace to transform our lives.

David's story and Aquinas's teachings challenge us to examine our own hearts. Are there sins we have hidden, even from ourselves? Are we willing to let the light of God's truth shine into our lives, even when it is uncomfortable?

The sacrament of reconciliation is a privileged encounter with God's mercy, where we, like David, can hear the words of forgiveness and begin anew. In confession, the same grace that restored David is offered to us: the grace to create a clean heart and renew a right spirit within us.

The story of David's sin and repentance is ultimately a story of hope. It shows us the depth of human weakness but also the greater depth of God's mercy. Saint Thomas Aquinas helps us understand that conversion is not merely about avoiding punishment but about returning to the source of all goodness and love.

May we, like David, have the courage to confront our sins, the humility to seek God's mercy, and the faith to trust in His grace. And may we, in our own lives, echo the words of David's psalm: *"Restore to me the joy of your salvation, and uphold me with a willing spirit"* (Psalm 51:12)

Twelfth Sunday in Ordinary Time

"For all of you who were baptized into Christ have clothed your-
selves with Christ. There is neither Jew nor Greek, there is neither slave
nor free person, there is not male and female; for you are all one in
Christ Jesus." (Galatians 3:27-28)

The passage from Galatians 3:26–29 is a profound declaration of
the unity and equality found in Christ. It speaks to the heart of our
Christian identity: through baptism, we become children of God,
clothed with Christ, and members of one body. Saint Paul proclaims
a radical truth that shatters the divisions of the ancient world and
offers a vision of unity and freedom that continues to challenge us
today.

In these verses, Paul addresses the Galatians' struggle with division, particularly over adherence to Jewish law. Some in the community argued that Gentile converts must follow the Mosaic law to
fully belong to God's people. Paul's response is unequivocal: faith in
Christ, not the law, is what makes us children of God.

Baptism marks the beginning of this new identity. To be "clothed
with Christ" means to take on His life, His values, and His mission.
It is a total transformation, where earthly distinctions—such as eth-
nicity, social status, and gender—are transcended in the unity of the
Body of Christ.

Paul's vision is not a denial of diversity but a celebration of unity
within diversity. In Christ, differences are not erased but integrated
into a greater whole, where every person is valued equally as a beloved child of God.

Saint Thomas Aquinas reflects deeply on the transformative power of grace in baptism. In his *Summa Theologiae*, he explains that baptism is the sacrament of spiritual regeneration, where the soul is cleansed of sin and elevated to participate in the divine life.

For Aquinas, the unity described in Galatians 3:28 is a direct result of this grace. Through baptism, we are united with Christ and with one another in a profound way that surpasses all human divisions. Aquinas teaches that this unity is rooted in charity, the highest virtue, which binds us to God and to our neighbors.

Aquinas also emphasizes that the distinctions Paul mentions—Jew or Greek, slave or free, male or female—are not abolished but reordered. In Christ, these distinctions no longer define our ultimate worth or separate us. Instead, they find their true purpose in service to the community and the glorification of God.

Pope Saint John Paul II often echoed Paul's message of unity in Christ, particularly in his teachings on human dignity and the universal call to holiness. In his encyclical *Redemptor Hominis*, he writes that Christ reveals the full meaning of humanity and the dignity of every person.

John Paul II saw baptism as the foundation of this dignity. By becoming children of God, we are called to recognize the divine image in every person, regardless of race, class, or gender. He tirelessly advocated for a culture of life and solidarity, where the unity of the human family in Christ overcomes the divisions caused by sin and selfishness.

Pope Francis frequently reflects on the unity and inclusivity of the Gospel. In *Fratelli Tutti*, he calls for a world where the recognition of our shared humanity leads to solidarity and care for one another. This vision resonates with Paul's declaration that we are all one in Christ Jesus.

Francis emphasizes that the Church, as the Body of Christ, must be a place where everyone feels welcomed and valued. He often speaks against forms of exclusion, whether based on race, economic status, or any other division, reminding us that in baptism, we are all equally beloved children of God.

Paul's message invites us to reflect on how we live out our baptismal identity in a world still marked by division and inequality. Are we living as children of God, clothed with Christ? Do we see others through the eyes of faith, recognizing their dignity as fellow members of the Body of Christ?

To live this unity requires more than words; it demands concrete action. It means breaking down barriers in our families, parishes, and communities. It means standing against racism, sexism, and other forms of injustice. It means building a culture of encounter, as Pope Francis often says, where we truly listen to and care for one another.

Galatians 3:26–29 is a powerful reminder of the gift and challenge of our baptismal identity. Saint Thomas Aquinas teaches us that this unity is a work of grace, transforming our hearts and binding us together in charity. Pope John Paul II calls us to recognize the dignity of every human person, while Pope Francis urges us to build a Church and a world that truly reflects this unity.

Let us strive to live as children of God, clothed with Christ, and committed to building a world where there is truly no Jew or Greek, slave or free, male or female, but all are one in Christ Jesus

Thirteenth Sunday in Ordinary Time

Elijah and Elisha

The readings we proclaim Sunday call me as a priest to examine my own vocation and the motivations that spur me onward to live this vocation wisely and well. The First Reading, taken from the First Book of Kings, details the story of Elijah finding Elisha and appointing him a prophet after Elijah is given this call of the Lord. The cloak of service is thrown over the young man and he is forced to make this radical change in his life, leaving all, including family, behind to serve the Lord.

Indeed, Saint Luke in the Gospel continues this theme. The Master encounters those who wish to follow him, to dedicate their lives to him, and they cannot do so. Unlike Elisha, they are ultimately too caught up in the things of this world, like family and property, all of them in themselves good. The Lord says: "No one who sets a hand to the plow and looks to what was left behind is fit for the kingdom of God." The refrain of the responsorial psalm reminds us: "You (God) are my inheritance, O Lord."

With all the trouble in the world, I contend that there has never been a better time to be a priest. Priests are more necessary than ever for the sanctifying of the world. What is necessary today for the priest is a radical reconfiguration to the Person to whom they were configured at their ordination — Jesus Christ, the Lord, the one, true, high priest.

For too long, I have forgotten that it is the Lord who is my sole inheritance, not human respect. For too long, I have set my hand to the plow and at least peered over my shoulder to see what is in back of me. The cloak of radical discipleship has been laid over us who are ordained priests. Therefore, in this age when we are called to be even more so agents of transparency — of healing, of trust, in the Church and the world — what are we to do?

Simple this — be Christ's priests. We were given the triple munera for ministry in the Church — to teach, to administer and to sanctify. If we are to live out this with our whole heart, mind and self, what a difference it would be for the Church and the world.

We are to teach and to preach the doctrine of the Church, not only what we think, or what we think might be best acceptable to society, but what our Mother the Church has entrusted to us in the Deposit of Faith without any alteration. This, of course, does not mean that we just recite the Catechism to the people to whom we serve, but it does mean that we understand, accept and teach the Church as it is authentically taught in the Magisterium. At all of our diaconal ordinations, we took an oath of fidelity. Those who are pastors and seminary formators and professors did as well. Now is the time, more than ever, for us to live up to it.

We are to administer the temporal goods of the Church with the sure and certain knowledge that it is not our property. We are merely the caretakers, those responsible for the goods and buildings and services which our Mother, the Church, has given to us as pastors.

We are called to sanctify the People of God, building up the Mystical Body of Christ by the reverent celebration of the sacraments, especially Holy Mass. Do we recognize that, when we offer the Holy Sacrifice of the Mass, it is Christ whom we call down in our own unworthy hands? Do we celebrate or concelebrate Holy Mass, even on days when we are not "on" to do so? Do we pray daily the Divine Office in its entirety, as we are obliged to do at our ordinations, not only for the sanctification of our own day, but in intercession for our Bride, the Church, for her growth in holiness? Do we make time daily for Eucharistic adoration, spending, indeed in the eyes of the world — wasting, time before our ultimate love?

The relationship for the priest that has to be primary is with God. He must realize that he is a beloved son of the Father and has to assure, through the formation of a "monasticism of the heart," becoming an active contemplative, that this relationship is primary. In the midst of a busy schedule, with all of its demands, I can understand how many of my brother priests could scoff at the concept of being an active contemplative. All one needs to do to be an active contemplative is to take the time daily for real, substantial prayer, preferably before the Blessed Sacrament, doing a daily examen.

From this relationship flows his identity, which is, by his ordination, configured to Christ, and he is ontologically, at the root of his being, changed. The priest is called to be the chaste spouse to the Church, married, if you will, to the Church, the Bride of Christ. He is called to be the spiritual father, the one who gives life to his people through his loving service, like any father to a family and by feeding them with the Eucharist. He is called to be the divine physician, healing his flock through the sacraments of penance and anointing of the sick. He is called to be head and shepherd, leading and guiding his flock even when the times get tough. What a noble role! What an honorable task! How could a priest with this understanding not be excited and want to set the world ablaze!

Fourteenth Sunday in Ordinary Time

In today's Gospel, taken from the Evangelist Luke, we read of the commissioning of the disciples by the Lord. We see that the Lord does something a little bit unusual and perhaps for our modern standards, a bit inefficient! He sends his disciples out two-by-two. Why would the Lord do this? With all the ground that He has to cover, with all the souls that need to hear the message of the Kingdom of God, why wouldn't He just send them out one-by-one? As one homilist once put years ago: "If these disciples can survive each other, they can survive anything the world, the flesh and the devil can throw at them!"

Yes, it is true that, at times, we can be our own worst enemies! How can we, all of whom are different and have radically different ideas and styles and ways of going about things, look beyond ourselves and pull it together so that the Church can grow? The first lesson to learn is that it's not about us; it's never about us; it's all about the Lord and how best we can serve him with our very lives.

This is an important lesson for all of us to remember when it comes to the nature of collegiality and cooperation on the parochial level, on the diocesan level and on the interdiocesan level. Sometimes, it doesn't matter where the souls, minds and hearts of the faithful are being formed and fed and who is doing the ministry; all that matters is that the souls, minds and hearts of the faithful are formed and fed.

On the parish level, how many of us have seen dedicated parishioners grow upset when one organization assists in accomplishing something for the parish that is traditionally "theirs?" When newer faces come to help and some of the long-time helpers in these various areas seem threatened, are we able to be like Christ and to reassure them that "whoever is not against us is for us?"

On the diocesan level, are we who are involved in the various ministries and apostolates in our own local parishes open and willing to collaborate with our neighboring parishes for the good of our people? If one of our local parishes is able to offer something that our resources, facility or staff can't, do we actively encourage it and promote it to our people? Or do we just start up our own version of it?

Discipleship in the Lord comes with the understanding that we are all, ultimately, as the Scriptures phrase it, "useless servants." We all need to pull together and sanctify the world by what we say and what we do. We speak so much of evangelization, of showing mercy to those outside the Church, those who might feel marginalized. There is an old expression of which I would like to remind us all: "Charity begins at home." If can give credible witness to the reality of our faith to each other, to other believers, to other practicing Catholics, then we surely can do so for the rest of the world. Jesus sends his disciples out, two by two. May we never forget his wisdom in doing so.

Fifteenth Sunday in Ordinary Time

In today's Gospel, we hear the parable of the Good Samaritan, one of the most well-known and impactful teachings of Jesus. The story is simple yet profound: A man is robbed, beaten, and left for dead on the side of the road. A priest and a Levite pass by, each ignoring the man's plight. But a Samaritan, a figure despised by the Jewish people of the time, stops to help the injured man, tending to his wounds and ensuring he receives care. Jesus concludes by asking, "Which of these three, do you think, was neighbor to the man who fell into the hands of robbers?" The answer, of course, is the one who showed mercy.

This parable invites us to reflect on the call to love our neighbor, a commandment we encounter repeatedly in Scripture. But it also challenges us to put that love into action, particularly through the corporal works of mercy, which are acts of kindness and service directed at addressing the physical needs of others. These works—feeding the hungry, giving drink to the thirsty, clothing the naked, welcoming the stranger, visiting the sick, visiting the imprisoned, and burying the dead—are not merely suggestions; they are concrete ways we live out the love of God for those in need.

Saint Thomas Aquinas, in his *Summa Theologiae*, provides deep insight into the theological foundations of mercy. He teaches that mercy is a central virtue that directs us toward the good of others, particularly in their suffering. Aquinas states that mercy is "the compassion of one person for another, by which one suffers with another in their distress." This is precisely what we see in the Good Samaritan: he does not merely feel pity for the man in need but acts decisively to alleviate his suffering. The Samaritan sees beyond any societal divisions or prejudices and, in doing so, exemplifies the very heart of mercy. For Aquinas, mercy is not a passive feeling; it is an active disposition that leads us to help those in need, regardless of their background or status.

Pope Francis, in his numerous writings and speeches, has emphasized the importance of mercy in the Christian life. In his *Bull of Indiction for the Jubilee of Mercy*, he writes, "Mercy is the fundamental law that dwells in the heart of every person who looks sincerely into the eyes of his brothers and sisters on the path of life." The Pope often speaks of mercy as something that must be lived concretely in our everyday actions. For him, the story of the Good Samaritan is a reminder that our love for our neighbor is not just a feeling, but a series of actions that involve personal sacrifice. Pope Francis frequently reminds us that mercy is especially necessary in the face of injustice, violence, and inequality—situations where it is easy to turn a blind eye, as the priest and Levite did in the parable.

In popular culture, we also encounter reflections of the Good Samaritan story. For instance, the film *The Pursuit of Happyness*, starring Will Smith, tells the true story of Chris Gardner, a man who struggles with homelessness while trying to provide a better life for his son. Despite his own difficulties, Gardner's compassion toward others—whether it's a fellow homeless person or a colleague at work—embodies the spirit of the Good Samaritan. The movie portrays not just the man's struggle but also his empathy for those around him, showing that mercy is not about wealth or status, but about a willingness to extend kindness and help to those in need, no matter the personal cost.

Similarly, the modern superhero genre, particularly through characters like Spider-Man, offers a popular take on the idea of mercy. The famous line from Uncle Ben, "With great power comes great responsibility," echoes the call of the Good Samaritan. Those with the ability to help others have a moral responsibility to act, even when it requires sacrifice. The image of the superhero stepping in to protect or help those in danger reflects the mercy of the Samaritan who acts despite societal divisions or personal inconvenience.

This parable and the works of mercy invite us to examine our own lives. How often do we pass by those in need, too preoccupied with our own concerns to notice the suffering of others? How easy it is to be like the priest or the Levite—good people, perhaps, but unwilling to take the necessary steps to help when it involves personal discomfort or inconvenience. But Jesus calls us to be like the Samaritan—to see with the eyes of mercy, to act with compassion, and to be a neighbor to all, regardless of their background or circumstance.

Let us ask ourselves: How can we better embody the works of mercy in our daily lives? It may not always involve grand gestures or dramatic acts, but often it is found in the small, everyday acts of kindness—feeding a hungry neighbor, offering a listening ear to someone in distress, visiting someone who is sick or lonely. Pope Francis reminds us that mercy is not a luxury for the few; it is a necessity for all. When we serve others with mercy, we are serving Christ, who told us, "Whatever you did for one of these least brothers of mine, you did for me" (Matthew 25:40).

As we receive the Eucharist today, let us remember that we are called not only to be the recipients of God's mercy but also its channels. May we leave this Mass with open eyes and open hearts, ready to serve those in need, and to show mercy to all, just as Christ has shown mercy to us.

Sixteenth Sunday in Ordinary Time

In today's readings from Genesis and Luke, we encounter two profound scenes that highlight the importance of hospitality, attentiveness, and the balance between service and contemplation. In the first reading, we see Abraham welcoming three mysterious visitors to his home, offering them food and shelter. In the Gospel, we see Jesus visiting the home of Martha and Mary, where Martha busily serves while Mary sits at the feet of Jesus, listening to his teachings. These stories invite us to reflect on how we are called to serve God and neighbor in both active and contemplative ways.

In Genesis 18:1-10a, we are told that Abraham, upon seeing three strangers, immediately offers them hospitality. He provides food, water, and shelter, demonstrating the virtue of hospitality, which in the ancient world was not merely a social custom but a sacred duty. Abraham's actions reveal the importance of welcoming the stranger, as this act of kindness is often seen in Scripture as a way of encountering God Himself. In fact, Christian tradition has understood this moment as a manifestation of the Trinity, with the three visitors symbolizing the three persons of the Father, Son, and Holy Spirit. Abraham's hospitality is not only an act of kindness but a prefiguration of the openness and receptivity that we must have to God in our lives.

Saint Thomas Aquinas, in his theological reflections, emphasizes that hospitality is an expression of charity, a virtue that seeks the good of others. In his *Summa Theologiae*, Aquinas writes that charity is not only about loving those who are close to us but also about extending love and care to strangers. Abraham's act of welcoming the visitors exemplifies this kind of charity. It shows us that, just as Abraham welcomed God into his home, we are called to welcome God into our lives, offering Him the hospitality of our hearts through acts of love, service, and generosity.

In the Gospel of Luke (10:38-42), we encounter the familiar scene of Jesus visiting the home of Martha and Mary. While Martha is busy with the tasks of serving and preparing for the guest, Mary sits at the feet of Jesus, listening attentively to His words. When Martha complains that Mary isn't helping, Jesus gently rebukes her, saying, "Martha, Martha, you are anxious and troubled about many things; one thing is necessary. Mary has chosen the good portion, which will not be taken away from her."

Jesus' words are often understood as highlighting the value of contemplation over mere activity. Martha represents the active life, the busyness of service and responsibility, while Mary embodies the contemplative life, a life centered on listening to the Word of God. Both are important, but Jesus reminds us that the contemplative life—the attention to God and His presence—is primary. In the end, service without a relationship with God can become mere busywork, while contemplation without action can lead to a lack of engagement with the world and its needs.

Aquinas, in his writings on the active and contemplative life, suggests that the two are not opposed but are meant to complement each other. In fact, he writes that contemplation is the higher form of life because it directly aligns with the pursuit of God. However, he also acknowledges the importance of action, particularly in the service of others. The key, according to Aquinas, is balance: the contemplative life must inform and inspire the active life, just as the active life should be directed toward the glory of God.

There is the need for both contemplation and action in the Christian life. We are called to be "not only doers of good works but also contemplators of the good." Our work and service should flow from our relationship with God, which is nourished by prayer and contemplation. Like Martha, we may be tempted to think that the busy work of life is more important, but when our lives are not rooted in the love and presence of God, even our best works can become hollow.

Jesus in the Gospel reminds us that our service, like that of Martha, must be rooted in our relationship with God, as exemplified by Mary. Without this balance, we risk becoming anxious and troubled about many things, just as Martha was. But when we take time to listen to God, as Mary did, we are grounded in the peace that comes from His presence, and our work becomes an expression of that peace and love.

So, how do these readings and reflections challenge us today? First, they invite us to practice hospitality—not just in the physical act of welcoming others but in the spiritual hospitality of making room for God in our hearts. Just as Abraham welcomed the three visitors, we are called to welcome Christ into our homes, into our lives, and into our hearts, not with superficial gestures but with a genuine openness that leads to a deep relationship with Him.

Second, we are called to reflect on the balance between service and contemplation. Are we too busy with the tasks of life, like Martha, that we forget to pause and listen to God's Word? Are we giving our time to the things that truly matter, or are we simply distracted by the many concerns of the world? Jesus calls us to find the "one thing necessary"—a deep and abiding relationship with Him that will guide and inspire all that we do.

Our works of service should flow from contemplation. Just as Martha's work was meant to serve Jesus, our actions in the world must flow from our relationship with God. The two—contemplation and action—are inseparable, each one enriching the other.

As we approach the altar today, let us ask for the grace to balance our lives, so that our service may be infused with the wisdom of God, and our contemplation may lead to acts of love and mercy in the world. May we welcome God into our hearts with the hospitality of Abraham, listen to His Word with the attentiveness of Mary, and serve others with the love and charity that flow from our relationship with Him.

Seventeenth Sunday in Ordinary Time

In today's readings, we are presented with two powerful moments of intercession and prayer. In the first reading from Genesis (18:20-32), we encounter the familiar story of Abraham negotiating with God for the fate of Sodom and Gomorrah. In the Gospel from Luke (11:1-13), we hear Jesus teaching His disciples how to pray, offering the Lord's Prayer and assuring them of God's generosity in answering prayers. Both readings speak to the nature of prayer, particularly the power of intercession and the generosity of God.

In Genesis 18:20-32, Abraham intercedes for the people of Sodom, asking God to spare the city if there are righteous people within it. Abraham's negotiation with God is remarkable—he begins by asking if God would spare the city for fifty righteous people, and then, in an act of boldness and humility, he continues to lower the number, down to ten. God agrees to spare the city for the sake of the righteous, even though, as the story unfolds, only Lot and his family are found to be righteous. This dialogue reveals much about the nature of prayer and intercession.

Saint Thomas Aquinas, in his *Summa Theologiae*, writes that one of the primary purposes of prayer is to participate in God's providence. When we pray, especially when we intercede for others, we are not changing God's will but aligning our hearts with His plan. In Abraham's case, his intercession demonstrates that God desires us to be involved in His saving work. While God knows all things and His will is perfect, He still welcomes our prayers and uses them to fulfill His plan. Abraham's persistence in asking for the city to be spared shows us the power of persistent prayer. The Fathers of the

Church, such as St. Augustine, echoed this understanding, teaching that God's providence allows our prayers to be part of the unfolding of His plan, even as He remains sovereign over all things.

In the Gospel of Luke, Jesus offers us the Lord's Prayer as the model for Christian prayer. When His disciples ask, "Lord, teach us to pray," Jesus provides them with the words we still pray today, "Our Father, who art in heaven…" This prayer contains both the elements of praise and petition, and it teaches us not only to address God as our Father but to trust that He is a loving Father who hears our needs and desires to give us what is good.

Saint Thomas Aquinas, in his commentary on the Lord's Prayer, explains that Jesus taught us this prayer to guide us in our relationship with God. The prayer encompasses both spiritual and material needs, and in doing so, it teaches us that prayer is not merely about our wants, but about aligning our desires with God's will. The "Our Father" reminds us of God's transcendence and immanence—He is both in heaven and intimately involved in our lives. Aquinas emphasizes that the petition "Give us this day our daily bread" reflects our dependence on God for both our physical and spiritual sustenance. This balance of humility and confidence in God's generosity is central to our Christian prayer life.

In the latter part of today's Gospel, Jesus reassures us that God is a generous Father who delights in giving good gifts to His children. He says, "If you then, who are evil, know how to give good gifts to your children, how much more will the heavenly Father give the Holy Spirit to those who ask Him!" Jesus emphasizes that, just as earthly parents desire to give good things to their children, God, our Father, desires even more to give us what is truly good. This is a call to confidence in prayer.

The Fathers of the Church, especially St. Augustine and St. John Chrysostom, taught that we must approach God with great trust, knowing that He loves us as His children. However, this does not mean that we will always receive what we ask for in the way we expect. Rather, we can be certain that God will give us what is best for us, even if it is not exactly what we requested. Prayer, then, is not about forcing God's hand, but about opening ourselves to His divine wisdom.

As we reflect on today's readings, we are invited to engage in prayer with both boldness and trust. Like Abraham, we are encouraged to intercede for others, persistently asking God for what is good and just, even if we do not understand why things happen the way they do. Like the disciples in the Gospel, we are taught to pray with confidence, knowing that our Father will give us what we need— especially the gift of the Holy Spirit, who empowers us to live as faithful children of God.

Let us approach God with the same persistence that Abraham showed, and the same trust that Jesus encourages us to have in the generosity of God. May we remember that, even in our most desperate moments, God is always listening, always willing to bless us with His presence and His grace. As we pray today, let us do so with the faith that God, our loving Father, will always provide for us, and that through prayer, we are drawn into a deeper relationship with Him.

Eighteenth Sunday in Ordinary Time

In today's first reading from Ecclesiastes (1:2; 2:21-23), we hear the famous refrain of the Preacher, "Vanity of vanities! All is vanity." The writer of Ecclesiastes is grappling with the reality of human life, and he declares that all human toil—work, striving, and effort—is ultimately futile. This is a stark reflection on the transient nature of existence, and it leads to the questions of why we work and what purpose our labor serves. We also hear in this passage how the fruits of labor, after a lifetime of toil, are often passed on to someone who did not labor for them, adding to the Preacher's sense of futility and dissatisfaction.

The theme of time—its fleeting nature and our relationship with it—is central to the reflections of Ecclesiastes. This leads us to think more deeply about how we understand time, and how we relate to it, both in human terms and in terms of God's eternal perspective.

In the Greek language, there are two distinct words for time: *chronos* and *kairos*. *Chronos* refers to the measurable, sequential passage of time—time as a series of moments, which we experience in the ticking of the clock, in days, years, and events that happen one after the other. *Kairos*, on the other hand, refers to the "appointed time," the opportune moment, or the "right time" for something to happen. *Kairos* is not measured by clocks or calendars but by the fullness of the moment, the divine timing that speaks to the deeper purpose of life.

In Ecclesiastes, we are confronted with *chronos*—the endless cycle of time in which human beings strive, work, and labor, only to see it pass away. The Preacher seems to be caught in a sense of *chronos* time, where all human effort appears futile in the face of death and the passage of generations. No matter how much one achieves, time renders it all meaningless. For the Preacher, *chronos* leads to cynicism—everything seems to be part of an endless, repetitive cycle, with no lasting significance.

However, Christian faith invites us to see beyond *chronos* and to enter into the perspective of *kairos*. Through the lens of faith, the seemingly futile struggles of *chronos* are not meaningless, for we know that there is a deeper, eternal plan in which God works. This is the perspective that allows us to see our lives not as an endless string of days but as part of God's larger, redemptive work.

The cynical tone of Ecclesiastes arises from the Preacher's realization that human labor often seems pointless, especially when faced with death. The Preacher wonders what is the point of working so hard, only for our efforts to be passed on to someone who may not appreciate them or continue the work in a meaningful way. This sense of futility can easily lead to despair or cynicism, where one sees no ultimate purpose in life and simply gives in to a sense of resignation.

Saint Thomas Aquinas, in his work *Summa Theologiae*, addresses the problem of meaning and purpose in human life. For Aquinas, the ultimate purpose of human life is union with God, the beatific vision. Unlike the Preacher in Ecclesiastes, Aquinas sees the efforts of human beings, even the struggles of daily life, as meaningful when they are oriented toward this ultimate end. For Aquinas, human beings are not meant to be trapped in the cyclical meaninglessness of *chronos*, but are called to live with the hope of *kairos*, the opportune moment when God's grace breaks into time and offers true fulfillment.

Aquinas would remind us that our work, even when it seems futile, can be a means of sanctification. Our human toil, when placed in the context of our relationship with God, is not futile; rather, it is part of the work of salvation. Just as Christ, the Word made flesh, entered into human history at a specific moment in time (*kairos*), our lives, too, are part of God's unfolding plan. The key is not to be absorbed in the passing moments of *chronos*, but to allow our hearts and actions to be open to the *kairos* moments where God's grace touches the present.

Hans Urs von Balthasar, a 20th-century Catholic theologian, offers a profound reflection on the relationship between time and eternity. For Balthasar, the central mystery of Christianity is that God, who is eternal, entered into the temporality of human history in the person of Jesus Christ. In Balthasar's view, the life, death, and resurrection of Jesus are the moments of *kairos* that give meaning to all of human *chronos*. Balthasar speaks of the "eternal now" of God's presence in Christ, where time and eternity meet in a way that transforms the meaning of every moment.

In the light of this, the Preacher's cynicism in Ecclesiastes can be addressed. If we view our lives through the lens of Christ's redemptive work, we are no longer caught in the despair of time's passing. Instead, our lives are caught up in God's eternal purpose, which makes every moment of time meaningful. The key is not to despair in the endless cycles of time but to recognize that Christ, through His Paschal Mystery, has given us the possibility of seeing every moment as part of His eternal love for us.

So, how can we live with a proper understanding of time? How do we live in a world where time seems fleeting, and yet we know that in Christ, every moment is filled with meaning? The answer is found in the tension between *chronos* and *kairos*. We must acknowledge the reality of time as we experience it—our daily struggles, our efforts, our work, and the apparent futility of all things under the sun. But we are also called to live with the eyes of faith, seeing in each moment the possibility of God's grace breaking through—God acting in the *kairos* of our lives, making every moment an opportunity for holiness, for communion with Him, and for bringing His love to the world.

In practical terms, this means that we should live our daily lives with purpose and intention, even while acknowledging the transience of earthly things. It means that, like Saint Thomas Aquinas teaches, we must direct our actions toward God and allow Him to sanctify them, so that even in the smallest tasks, we are participating in His eternal plan. And like Balthasar's vision of Christ, we must open ourselves to the transformative power of the "eternal now" that touches our present moment with grace.

As we continue with this Mass, let us place our lives before God, acknowledging the passing nature of time while also opening ourselves to the eternal grace of God that fills every moment with purpose. May we live in the light of *kairos*, trusting that our work and our lives, no matter how fleeting, are caught up in the eternal plan of love that God has for us.

Nineteenth Sunday in Ordinary Time

At the risk of dating myself, the first U.S. president of whom I was conscious was Jimmy Carter. I seem to have vague recollections of the hostages being held in Iran and that Carter was the President. Most likely, I knew who the President was through my older siblings telling me of Dan Aykroyd's impressions of Carter on *Saturday Night Live*. Whatever one may think of Carter's politics, one can hardly argue that he isn't a strong practicing Christian man.

Former President Carter tells the story of his days working with Admiral Hyman Rickover when he was a young officer in the U.S. Navy. Carter states he learned a valuable life lesson from this experience:

"I had applied for the nuclear submarine program, and Admiral Rickover was interviewing me for the job. It was the first time I met Admiral Rickover, and we sat in a large room by ourselves for more than two hours, and he let me choose any subjects I wished to discuss. Very carefully, I chose those about which I knew most at the time--current events, seamanship, music, literature, naval tactics, electronics, gunnery--and he began to ask me a series of questions of increasing difficulty. In each instance, he soon proved that I knew relatively little about the subject I had chosen. He always looked right into my eyes, and he never smiled. I was saturated with cold sweat. Finally he asked a question and I thought I could redeem myself. He said, "How did you stand in your class at the Naval Academy?" Since I had completed

my sophomore year at Georgia Tech before entering Annap-
olis as a plebe, I had done very well, and I swelled my chest
with pride and answered, "Sir, I stood fifty-ninth in a class of
820!" I sat back to wait for the congratulations--which never
came. Instead, the question: "Did you do your best?" I started
to say, "Yes, sir," but I remembered who this was and recalled
several of the many times at the Academy when I could have
learned more about our allies, our enemies, weapons, strat-
egy, and so forth. I was just human. I finally gulped and said,
"No, sir, I didn't always do my best." He looked at me for a
long time, and then turned his chair around to end the interview. He asked one final question, which I have never been
able to forget--or to answer. He said, "Why not?" I sat there
for a while, shaken, and then slowly left the room."

The basic message of Mr. Carter's story, namely always try your
best, always give 100% of yourself, can also be a message which we
can glean from the Gospel this Sunday taken from the Evangelist
Luke. The Lord Jesus speaks of the "wise and prudent steward"
whom the master has placed in charge of the household to distribute
the food allowance at the proper time. Our Saviour states univocally:
"Much will be required of the person entrusted with much, and still
more will be demanded of the person entrusted with more."

As Catholics, we have been entrusted with very much. We have
been given the gift of faith by the Lord Jesus Christ and the consola-
tion of the Truth by the Holy Spirit. By the will and the love of the
God the Father, we live and move and have our being. Through our
Mother, the Church, we are fed with the finest of nourishment, the
Real Presence of Christ in the Eucharist. Through her, we receive the

other life-giving sacraments and learn of the Way of the Lord Jesus. We have indeed been given much. A question, then: what are we doing with what we have been given by the Lord and the Church?

In my role as a professor of theology for seminarians, I am charged with directing the intellectual formation of our seminarians. I know that I can't give them what I don't have. Therefore, I can't rest on my laurels. I need to continue to study, to prepare, to research and write, so that I can serve them and continue to be an example of a diocesan priest actively engaged in the intellectual life of the Church. I need to continually update my lectures and classes and never be satisfied with something that I had done a long time ago and never updated. I tell the seminarians that they don't have to be geniuses; that's not what the Church necessarily needs; however, what they all need to do is give 100% of themselves over to their studies, to try their absolute best, to strive for excellence in knowledge the same way that a young medical intern would have to do so, because, ultimately they will be doctors of the soul, spiritual surgeons, dealing with the supernatural healing necessary for the most important thing in the world- the salvation of souls. Don't do it just for good grades; do it because the People of God need you to know your stuff.

What do we do with the gift of our faith? Have we continued to grow in knowledge of our faith, of Sacred Scripture, of the teachings of the Church, or have we allowed our own faith formation to cease once we have received the Sacrament of Confirmation? Our Diocese School of Evangelization helps guides our local Directors of Faith Formation in every parish to offer some wonderful resources for the increase in knowledge of the faith and love of the Lord.

Have we continued to grow in our spiritual lives? Do we make the time, even if it's just a few moments, for prayer? What is prayer? Prayer is a conversation with the One who loves us the most, our Lord. If we can't devote a great deal of time to prayer in our busy daily schedule, perhaps we might practice the art of becoming more aware of the presence of God in our daily lives. What do I mean by this?

Here's some suggestions: when we wake, take a brief moment and tell the Lord thanks for bringing us to a new day and dedicate our thoughts, works, joys, and sufferings to his greater glory. During the day, stop when we have a break and offer an Our Father, a Hail Mary, and a Glory be for all those who just can't for whatever reason (persecution, sickness, etc.) pray. At the end of the day, take a moment and thank the Lord for the good things of the day and ask him for forgiveness for time we have failed. Really simple, really basic, and this little practice of awareness usually will take no more than three minutes!

For those who wish to do more, the Church offers us her liturgy in the Holy Mass and the Divine Office, the official prayer of the Church. The Holy Rosary is a simple and reliable way to practice contemplative prayer. An Examen, coming from the spirituality of Saint Ignatius Loyola, is a wonderful way to grow in knowledge of God and self. And, if we can, we can spend some time before the Mirror of Truth that is the Blessed Sacrament. These are just some simple ways to avoid becoming spiritually "flabby," little ways in which we can hopefully grow to a mature spiritual relationship with Christ.

We indeed have been given much by the Lord and, indeed, much is required. May we become in our vocations in life as laity, consecrated persons, and clergy more and more those wise and faithful stewards described by our Lord in today's Gospel. May we always give 100% to Christ and his Bride, the Church.

Twentieth Sunday in Ordinary Time

I had the opportunity in the summer of 2016 to study at Creighton University in Omaha, Nebraska. I was enrolled for the three and a half week program for seminary faculty members sponsored by the Institute for Priestly Formation, which is based out of Creighton. To be honest, Omaha was not quite what I expected. I was thinking corn field upon corn field and instead found a busy, modern, gentrified city, bustling with activity from the College World Series and the U.S. Olympic Swimming try-outs. I also did not expect the oppressive heat!

When I first arrived at Creighton, the air-conditioning in the room where I was staying was not functioning and it was about 100 degrees outside! The kind staff of the University quickly remedied the situation, but it was still oppressively hot. One day, I took a long walk around the campus and found an impressive monument, one that was beautifully appropriate for a Jesuit university- an perpetual flame with an inscription of the words of the founder of the Society of Jesus, Saint Ignatius Loyola: "*Ite Inflammate Omnia*," "Go, set the world ablaze." These words, of course, were inspired by the words of the Lord Jesus taken from today's Gospel from the Evangelist Luke: "I have come to set the earth on fire, and how I wish it were already blazing!"

Being inflamed with the love of the Lord should be the goal of each and every Christian. By our words and our actions, we need to set the earth on fire. We have the Good News! We share in the Life, the Eternal Life that is our Lord, Jesus Christ. We are washed clean in the Precious Blood of the Lamb of God who has come to take our sins away. We are made in Christ a New creation. We should be on fire with the message, the basic kerygma, as we said in the former translation of the Mass in English- "Christ has died, Christ has risen, Christ will come again." And yet, if we were to go to some parishes on a Sunday morning, being on fire for the Lord would be the last thing of which we as Catholics would be accused.

Some of our parishes can seem like a wet blanket has been wrapped around them. They can seem dull, lifeless, joyless. We have Jesus Christ, fully present sacramentally in the Eucharistic species! The Lord is present and we have the honor to receive him, have him enter into our bodies and souls in the Eucharist, becoming our food, becoming our nourishment. He allows himself to be transformed and become part of us. And yet, at the elevation of the Most Blessed Sacrament, the Real Presence of Christ is welcomed not with the ringing of the Sanctus bells or with the private evocation of "My Lord and My God," but with a yawn!

How can we reignite the fire with which the Lord has blessed us? How can we set fire to the word by our thoughts, words, and actions as Christians? May I suggest a way, coming from an old axiom, taken from Saint Augustine of Hippo: "You cannot love what you do not know."

"You cannot love what you do not know." Let's apply this to the entire congregation of the average Church on a Sunday morning, breaking it down into three basic elements: the priest, the People of God, and the Eucharist.

First, the priest- What's really the biggest crisis facing the priesthood today? It's not broken ordination promises, necessarily; it's not clerical sexual abuse; at its essence, the biggest issue is the lack of a true and real priestly identity. It's about knowing who a priest is supposed to be. And if a priest doesn't understand who he is and what he is supposed to be, then how can he lead the people of God as head and shepherd? How can he inspire vocations to the priesthood and religious life?

The priest is not a functionary. The priest is not mainly a facilitator of the ministries of others in the community. One of the basic messages of the summer program, the Institute for Priestly Formation, is this idea. The priest must reorder his entire being, his entire worldview around the idea of relationship with God, then identity in Christ, and then his mission. Many problems, particularly burn-out, resentment of his mission, and an overfunctionality, occur when the priest gets the order confused. For myself at times (and dare I say for many of my brother priests), I have reversed the order, placing mission first, getting the job done, at the expense of relationship and identity.

The relationship for the priest that has to be primary is with God. He must realize that he is a beloved son of the Father and has to assure, through the formation of a "monasticism of the heart," becoming an active contemplative, that this relationship is primary. In the midst of a busy schedule, with all of its demands, I can understand how many of my brother priests could scoff at the concept of being an active contemplative. All one needs to do to be an active contemplative is to take the time daily for real, substantial prayer, preferably before the Blessed Sacrament, doing a daily examen.

From this relationship flows his identity, which is, by his ordination, configured to Christ, and he is ontologically, at the root of his being, changed. The priest is called to be the chaste spouse to the Church, married, if you will, to the Church, the Bride of Christ. He is called to be the spiritual father, the one who gives life to his people

through his loving service, like any father to a family and by feeding
them with the Eucharist. He is called to be the divine physician, healing his flock through the sacraments of penance and anointing of
the sick. He is called to be head and shepherd, leading and guiding
his flock even when the times get tough. What a noble role! What an
honorable task! How could a priest with this understanding not be
excited and want to set the world ablaze!

Second, the People of God- what's their identity? They are, by
baptism, a priestly people, different than the ordained, ministerial
priesthood, but in the primary sacrament of initiation, they share in
that priesthood. They offer, as the old morning offering prayer, goes
their "prayers, works, joys, and sufferings in union with the Holy
Sacrifice of the Mass throughout the world." They are to be leaven
in the world- to be the very presence of Christ in their homes, their
families, their workplaces. They are to be actively engaged, not only
in the liturgy, not only in their liturgical functions, but primarily
through their apostolic charitable works. It is their task to bring the
Jesus whom the priest consecrates on the altar to the world, not only
if they happen to serve as an extraordinary minister of Holy Communion, but mostly in how they act as ministers of mercy, agents of
God's saving justice to everyone whom they encounter. The Mass is
not merely a passive exercise for the congregation, with only the
priest and those involved in liturgical functions involved. Everyone
is involved, learning from the words of the Word of Life and feeding
on his Body and Blood so as to be transformed by him. What a noble
role! What an honorable task! How could a member of the priestly
people of the Body of Christ not be excited with this understanding
and not want to set the world ablaze!

Third, the Eucharist- what is it? Or rather who is it? It is not a sign, not a symbol, not just a nice thing to do, a sharing of food and fellowship. No, it is Jesus, he who is fully God and fully man, sacramentally present to us under the form of bread which is no longer bread, but his Precious Body, and wine, which is no longer wine but his Precious Blood. At the Mass, on that altar, Heaven and Earth kiss and we are transformed! With this understanding, how could all of us, priests and people alike, not be excited.

Saint Ignatius Loyola, the founder of the Jesuits, was a young soldier, inspired by tales of chivalry and adventure. During the recovery after the accident in which he was seriously injured, he was inspired by the nobility of the saints, particularly Dominic and Francis. When we gather to celebrate the Holy Mass, we are involved in the most noble task, the greatest adventure this side of Heaven. Once we recall who we are and what we are meant to be, we can recognize again this adventure. May we never lose sight of how our Sunday Eucharist can set us ablaze!

Twenty-First Sunday in Ordinary Time

I remember it like it was yesterday. It is a day whose memory remains with me forever! It was the day that I received my first and only detention at Cathedral Prep Seminary, Elmhurst, in 1989. As a high school junior, I was asked to "lend" my French homework to a fellow student and I promptly obliged. Our instructor, a bright young lady, upon examination of my homework and that of my "neighbor" quickly realized that something was amiss and I was served a detention! Here was I, the Student Council President, the Head Sacristan, having to stay after school in the classroom of the Prefect of Students. Oh, the shame! The ignominy of it all! I could barely hold my head up high as a Cathedralite! I had let down everyone- my classmates, my beloved school, the priests of Cathedral, and, above all, myself.

As you could tell, I was a bit dramatic back then (I probably still am!), but I really learned my lesson. In that forty minute period in room 303, I was on the fringes of society, I was a felon, doing "hard time." I know it wasn't a major thing at all, but it was for a 16 year old. When I was blessed to teach at Cathedral for my eight years there, I was very careful when I gave a detention (I think from 2004-2012, I only gave three detentions!)

The epistle we proclaim this Sunday from the Letter to the Hebrews reminds us all about discipline: ""My son, do not disdain the discipline of the Lord or lose heart when reproved by him; for whom the Lord loves, he disciplines; he scourges every son he acknowledges." Endure your trials as "discipline"; God treats you as sons. For what "son" is there whom his father does not discipline? At the time, all discipline seems a cause not for joy but for pain, yet later it brings the peaceful fruit of righteousness to those who are trained by it.""

Being corrected stinks! It's awful! It's embarrassing! No matter what age one is, no matter what state in life a person has, no one enjoys being told that what he or she is doing is wrong! And yet, if we are open, attentive, reasonable, loving, and honest, we can and should learn from being disciplined.

Let's examine the concept of discipline on the natural and the supernatural level, for the natural always leads to our understanding of the Divine life on the supernatural level. On the natural level, we can examine the one who is required to correct and the one who is corrected.

My high school principal, years later when I first began to teach at Cathedral, told me that the entire year is over in terms of classroom management by Columbus Day. By October, the students know what the teacher expects and the teacher knows what the students expect. If the teacher does not establish himself or herself as firm, but fair, being balanced, not being arbitrary, then that academic year more or less will be lost. It's hard to reroute the ship in mid-course.

Teachers, parents, employers are all required, in justice, to establish clear codes of discipline. It's not fun, it's not easy, but if we are to love those who have been entrusted to us, then we must, at times, discipline. It can never be cowardly or cruel, never out of vengeance or annoyance, never out of pride or hurt feelings; if an action of discipline must take place, it has to take place with two things in mind. First, the good of the individual- what message will the one who has committed the offense learn if no action is taken? Little infractions invariably lead to greater ones later and greater harm can come to those who never are corrected when they are wrong, especially when they are young. Second, the good of the greater community- what lesson is transmitted to the greater group when those responsible look the other way and do nothing when an offense has taken place? It often can lead to others following and emulating that bad example and it can also lead to a lack of morale and a lack of faith and trust in leadership on the part of the greater community.

This is also true when it comes to fraternal correction. Yes, it is true that nothing is as odious as fraternal correction, but it is, at times, necessary. The same rules apply, with the one having to do the fraternal correction always asking himself his intentions and using the actions of the other as a mirror, recognizing that he or she himself is not perfect either and needs to grow.

If this is true concerning discipline on the natural level, so too is it true on the supernatural level. Like a good teacher, like a gentle father, God takes no joy in correcting us. He does not delight in our infractions and wait to spring on us so that he can "slap us down." No, God is full of love and mercy. God's purest nature, who God is at his essence, is Love. The concrete application of love is mercy, a lesson that Pope Francis has striven to teach us in the Extraordinary Jubilee of Mercy. Following this logic, the correct application of mercy is justice. And justice, because of our fallen human nature, tainted by original sin, has to lovingly be applied to situations in which we are hurting ourselves in sin and participating in situations that are explicitly evil.

Just as God the Father orders all things in the universe according to his eternal law, he has created all things to live in natural law. The Church, as loving Mother, establishes ecclesiastical law for the growth of each member of the Body of Christ and for the well-being of the Church as a whole. The discipline of the Church concerning such things like the sacraments are not meant to be burdensome, but meant to help the People of God grow in holiness, truth, and integrity.

So, a question then for us who hold the Catholic faith- do we know what the Church teaches on issues? Do we try to find out what is actually being taught definitively by the Church? Do we ask questions of those who know or do we allow the secular media to inform our opinions, even when they can (and often do) get the entire message wrong? And a further question, one especially for those of us who are clergy or in consecrated life and for those in the Church whose apostolate is to catechize- do we teach, clearly, objectively, and without any spin, what the Church teaches? Do we ourselves know what the Church is teaching and have offered up our time to keep ourselves up to date on the official teaching of the Church?

Discipline can be a tough thing, both to receive and to give. However, each of us at various points of our lives is called to receive it and give it, and, usually, it is for our own good. In the case of the discipline of the Lord, it is always for our good, our ultimate good, namely our salvation. It's what makes us beloved sons and daughters. May we learn to trust our loving Father in Heaven and our Mother, the Church in their efforts to discipline us as their children.

Twenty-Second Sunday in Ordinary Time

In today's Gospel from Saint Luke, we encounter a profound teaching on humility. Jesus, at a banquet, observes the guests choosing places of honor and offers a simple but powerful lesson: "For everyone who exalts himself will be humbled, and the one who humbles himself will be exalted" (Luke 14:11). In this teaching, Jesus invites us to adopt a posture of humility, one that recognizes the true value of our human dignity in the light of God's grace, not through the lens of worldly recognition or self-promotion.

To understand this Gospel more deeply, let's turn to the wisdom of three great figures of the Church—Pope Francis, Saint Thomas Aquinas, and Saint John Paul II—and also draw some inspiration from film and art.

Pope Francis has consistently taught us about the importance of humility. In his apostolic exhortation *Evangelii Gaudium*, he speaks of the Church's mission as one of humility and service, not power and prestige. He writes, "The Church is called to come out of herself and go to the peripheries, not to place herself at the center." In this, Pope Francis embodies the humility that Christ speaks of: not seeking power or honor for its own sake, but rather humbling oneself in service to others. His life and papacy provide a living example of how we are to embrace humility, especially in our relationships with the marginalized, the poor, and the forgotten.

Saint Thomas Aquinas, in his theological reflections, reminds us that humility is the foundation of all virtue. In his *Summa Theologiae*, he explains that humility is the virtue that moderates our sense of self-importance, aligning it with the reality that all we have is a gift from God. Aquinas argues that humility is not about thinking less of ourselves, but thinking of ourselves less—recognizing that our true worth comes from God alone. Humility, therefore, allows us to serve others without seeking glory or recognition. It is the virtue that enables us to live the commandment of love fully, because it teaches us to look beyond ourselves to the needs of others.

Saint John Paul II also gave us a powerful witness of humility throughout his pontificate. Despite his towering intellectual and spiritual accomplishments, he remained a man of great humility, always focusing on the dignity of the human person and the need for service to others. In his encyclical *Redemptor Hominis*, he emphasizes that Jesus Christ, in his humility, shows us the true meaning of greatness: "The human person is the way of the Church," he writes, highlighting that true greatness is found in self-giving love, not in worldly power or acclaim. Pope John Paul II's life itself, with his constant efforts to reach out to all people, particularly the oppressed and suffering, exemplified the kind of humility Christ taught.

When we look at the world of film and art, we also find poignant examples of humility. One such example is the film *The Mission*, which tells the story of Jesuit priests in South America who serve and protect indigenous people. The central figure, Father Gabriel, played by Jeremy Irons, is a man who gives up personal ambition to serve a people on the margins. His ultimate act of humility is seen in the self-sacrificial way he lays down his life for others. The film portrays the paradox of humility: in giving up power and prestige, Father Gabriel finds the true meaning of love and service, much as Christ did on the cross.

Another example can be seen in the painting *The Supper at Emmaus* by Caravaggio. In this iconic image, we see the humble moment of revelation when the risen Christ is recognized by the disciples only after he serves them at the table. In this scene, Christ's humility is powerfully expressed—not as a distant, untouchable figure, but as one who shares in the most human of experiences. The disciples' recognition of him becomes not just a spiritual epiphany, but also a moment of deep humility as they understand that the risen Christ is present in the simplest acts of service and love.

Jesus' words to us today, then, are not just about our actions but about the posture of our hearts. Humility, as Pope Francis, Aquinas, and John Paul II teach us, is not an act of self-deprecation but a recognition of the truth—that we are all beloved children of God, dependent on His grace. Humility allows us to love others as Christ loves us, without seeking reward or recognition. It is in the humble service of others that we find our true dignity and, as Christ promised, we are ultimately exalted by God, not because of any self-promotion, but because of our willingness to serve as Christ served.

In this Eucharist, let us pray for the grace to embrace the humility of Christ, to choose the lowest seat, not out of false modesty but out of a deep awareness of our dependence on God and our call to serve others. May our lives reflect the humility of the saints and of Christ himself, who, though he was in the form of God, humbled himself to become one of us, even to the point of death on a cross.

Twenty-Third Sunday in Ordinary Time

The Gospel we proclaim today from the Evangelist Luke's 14th chapter can really seem harsh. The Lord Jesus actually wants is to hate our families and even our own life? What does he mean? The Lord Jesus then asks us to embrace our own cross, and, please recall that this is before his own Passion, so, for the disciples hearing this, he is asking them to embrace not a symbol of triumph over sin and death, a sign of the Lord's endless love, but, in fact, the very symbol of the worst, most shameful death that could be inflicted on a person in the Roman world. In fact, according to Jewish law, Christ redeemed us from the curse of the law by becoming a curse for us— for it is written, "Cursed is everyone who is hanged on a tree." This is found in Saint Paul's letter to the Galatians 3:13. Then, after speaking about proper and prudent planning, the Lord Jesus then says to his disciples, and by extension, to us, in today's Gospel, that we must renounce all our possessions in order to be his disciple.

What is the Lord Jesus actually telling us in his exhortation today? What does the Lord really want from us? Perhaps only this- to make the Lord and the Lord alone the center of our life. He is asking us more than anything to refocus our spiritual eyesight, to move from our spiritual myopia and readjust our vision to focus on what truly matters, namely the Lord and the things of the Lord.

In considering the words of Jesus in this Gospel passage, it's important to reflect on the profound call to discipleship that he is giving us. This is no ordinary invitation. It is a radical summons to reorder our lives in such a way that Christ is not just part of the picture, but the center, the axis around which everything else revolves. This demand for total devotion, even to the point of "hating" one's family or one's own life, might seem extreme, yet it is not about literal hatred but about prioritizing the love for Christ above all else, even our deepest attachments.

Hans Urs von Balthasar, in his reflections on discipleship, points out that this is not a call to escape from the world or from relationships, but rather to allow the love of Christ to so permeate our hearts that it redefines every relationship. Balthasar emphasizes that true discipleship requires us to live in the world but not be of it. The challenge here is to love others rightly—through the love of Christ. As we are invited to take up our cross, we are also invited to see in that cross the perfect expression of God's love for the world. This love does not seek power or status but chooses to suffer for the good of others. Discipleship, then, is not about our own glory but about the glory of God, and the sacrifice we make in following Christ is not a loss but a gain, for in giving up everything, we find everything.

Pope Benedict XVI, reflects similarly on this in his teachings on Christian discipleship. He writes that the cross is the ultimate sign of God's commitment to humanity. Discipleship, he explains, is a journey that involves a continual dying to oneself. The cross, while a symbol of suffering, is also a symbol of transformation—death leading to new life. For Ratzinger, the call to take up one's cross is a call to embrace the daily suffering that comes with living the Gospel in a fallen world, not with a grim resignation, but with the hope that this suffering will bear fruit. Discipleship, in this view, is not about fleeing suffering but accepting it as part of our participation in the redemptive work of Christ.

Finally, Dietrich Bonhoeffer, a Lutheran martyr of the faith who lived in a time of intense political and personal crisis, provides a very concrete example of what it means to follow Christ at all costs. In his book *The Cost of Discipleship*, Bonhoeffer famously writes that "when Christ calls a man, he bids him come and die." For Bonhoeffer, discipleship was about taking the risk of radical obedience to Christ, even when it meant conflict with the powers of the world, even when it led to persecution or death. His words echo the Gospel message we hear today: discipleship demands a detachment from all that is not Christ, a willingness to renounce not only material possessions but also personal safety, social status, and even family ties, in order to follow Jesus wherever he leads.

What all these thinkers remind us is that discipleship is not about what we stand to gain in earthly terms, but about participating in the life, death, and resurrection of Christ. To be his disciple is to give our hearts wholly to him, to place him at the center of our lives, so that everything else flows from that relationship. This might seem like a call to embrace the negative, the painful, the costly, but it is ultimately a call to life—abundant life, eternal life. As we take up our crosses, we are invited into a deeper union with Christ, and in this union, we find not just the meaning of our suffering, but the meaning of our very existence.

In light of all this, we can ask ourselves: Are we willing to let Christ be the center of our lives, not as a part of our agenda but as the very reason for it? Are we ready to embrace the cross that comes with following him, knowing that through that cross, we are drawn into the very heart of God's love for the world? Beg the Lord to give us the grace to focus on him above all things, to see him as the treasure of our hearts, and to follow him without reservation, wherever he may lead.

Twenty-Fourth Sunday in Ordinary Time

The Gospel for today offers us three powerful parables from Luke 15: the Lost Sheep, the Lost Coin, and the Prodigal Son. Together, they reveal the boundless mercy of God, a mercy that seeks, finds, forgives, and rejoices. These stories challenge us to reflect on God's love, our own hearts, and the call to embody divine mercy in our lives.

The parable of the Lost Sheep opens with a question: *"What man among you having a hundred sheep and losing one of them would not leave the ninety-nine in the desert and go after the lost one until he finds it?"* The image of the shepherd who seeks the lost sheep reveals God's merciful initiative. He does not wait for us to find Him but comes searching for us.

Saint Thomas Aquinas describes mercy as the highest expression of love, saying: *"Mercy is heartfelt sympathy for another's distress, impelling us to help them if we can. It is rooted in love and manifests the perfection of charity"* (*Summa Theologiae*, II-II, Q.30, Art.1).

In the Good Shepherd, we see divine mercy embodied. He risks everything to save the one lost sheep, showing that each person is precious in God's eyes.

The parable of the Lost Coin emphasizes the tireless effort of God to reclaim what is lost. Just as the woman sweeps the house and searches diligently, so does God pursue us, never giving up until we are restored to Him.

Pope Francis frequently reminds us of this relentless mercy. In *Evangelii Gaudium*, he writes: *"The Gospel invites us to rejoice at the shepherd who finds the lost sheep, the woman who recovers her coin. The heart of God is like this: He rejoices more when one sinner returns than over ninety-nine righteous ones who have no need of repentance"* (*EG*, 3). God's mercy is not passive; it is active and searching, reflecting His infinite love for every soul.

The parable of the Prodigal Son brings the theme of mercy to its climax. The younger son, after squandering his inheritance, comes to his senses and decides to return to his father, not as a son but as a servant. Yet the father's response exceeds all expectations. He runs to embrace his son, clothes him with dignity, and celebrates his return.

Saint Augustine beautifully captures the father's love, saying: *"God is more anxious to bestow His blessings on us than we are to receive them."* The father does not scold or punish but restores the son to his rightful place in the family. Pope Francis, reflecting on this parable, Pope Francis has called it the "icon of mercy," saying: *"The father's joy symbolizes the joy of God for every sinner who returns to Him and asks for forgiveness. It is the joy of a father who does not remember the sins or ingratitude of his child, but who rejoices because the child is back in his arms."*(*Misericordiae Vultus*, 9).

The elder son's reaction challenges us to examine our own hearts. He resents his father's mercy and refuses to join the celebration. How often do we begrudge God's forgiveness of others? Do we see ourselves as more deserving of His love?

Saint Thérèse of Lisieux reminds us: *"If you are willing to bear serenely the trial of being displeasing to yourself, then you will be for Jesus a pleasant place of shelter."* We must acknowledge our need for mercy and extend it to others, remembering that God's love is not a limited resource.

The parables of Luke 15 are not just about God's mercy but also a call to action. If we have received mercy, we are called to share it. Saint Thomas Aquinas teaches that mercy perfects justice because it transforms judgment into love.

In our lives, we are called to be like the shepherd who seeks the lost, the woman who searches diligently, and the father who forgives unconditionally. As Pope Francis says: *"Mercy is the bridge that connects God and humanity, opening our hearts to the hope of being loved forever despite our sinfulness."* (*Misericordiae Vultus*, 2).

This week, let us reflect on these questions: first, who in our lives needs to experience God's mercy through us? Second, how can we embody the searching, persistent, and unconditional love of God? The parables end with a celebration, a heavenly rejoicing over one sinner who repents. As we draw closer to Christ, let us echo that joy, celebrating not only the mercy we have received but also the mercy we are called to give. May the example of saints like Augustine, Thérèse, and Aquinas inspire us to live as instruments of God's boundless love, drawing others into His infinite embrace.

Twenty-Fifth Sunday in Ordinary Time

In the Gospel we proclaim this morning from the Evangelist Luke, we hear a familiar line from the Lord Jesus:

> "No servant can serve two masters.
> He will either hate one and love the other,
> or be devoted to one and despise the other.
> You cannot serve both God and mammon."

As Christians, men and women who are fully initiated members of the Church, we are called to be in the world and yet not of the world. We are incorporated into the Mystical Body of Christ, the Church, and, as such, we have to make decisions, ones either for Christ and his Church or against Christ and his Church.

Perhaps like many of you, I am Jesuit-trained. My bachelors, masters, and doctoral degrees in sacred theology all come from a Jesuit university, although I am proud to say that I went to a high school run by diocesan priests and I went to St. John's University in Queens for my BA in English. The Examen prayer and Imaginative prayer, which are hallmarks of Ignatian spirituality, are major parts of my daily prayer life and I could not imagine not praying in this manner.

Saint Ignatius Loyola, the founder of the Society of Jesus (more commonly known as the Jesuits) in his Spiritual Exercises speaks of "The Two Standards": the way of the Lord Jesus or the way of the world. By his use of the term "standard," Ignatius means a banner under which a regiment marches. We as Christians have to make a choice!

When we choose to live as a standard bearer for Christ, we recognize who Christ is and who we are. We recognize, in utter, complete, total humility, that God is God and that we are not. We are creatures and God is creator, and that everything we have and possess is a gift, freely given, of God to us. As Georges Bernanos, the French Catholic author wrote in his famous novel, *Diary of a Country Priest*, "All is grace!" Indeed all is grace!

Once we choose God over mammon, once we pick the things of the Lord over the things of his world, the haze of self-deception is lifted. And as Christ did, we recognize that we live not for ourselves, but for Christ and for others. Our response to the gratuitous gift of God that is our very existence is not a concern for "What's in it for me"? but a call to see God in all things, as the Jesuit poet Gerard Manley Hopkins wrote in his poem "As Kingfishers Catch Fire:"

As kingfishers catch fire, dragonflies draw flame;
As tumbled over rim in roundy wells
Stones ring; like each tucked string tells, each hung bell's
Bow swung finds tongue to fling out broad its name;
Each mortal thing does one thing and the same:
Deals out that being indoors each one dwells;
Selves — goes itself; *myself* it speaks and spells,
Crying *Whát I dó is me: for that I came.*

I say móre: the just man justices;
Keeps grace: thát keeps all his goings graces;
Acts in God's eye what in God's eye he is —

Christ — for Christ plays in ten thousand places,
Lovely in limbs, and lovely in eyes not his
To the Father through the features of men's faces.

Having become able to see Christ in all things, we then recognize that we are to be the heart, the hands, and the voice of Christ in the world, especially to the poor, the weak, the forgotten, and the oppressed. We are commissioned as the standard bearers of Christ Jesus to become men and women for others, which is the purpose of a Jesuit education. Fr. Pedro Arrupe, a former Father General of the Jesuits, who is coming closer and closer to canonization, wrote way back in 1973:

> "Today our prime educational objective must be to form men-and-women-for-others; men and women who will live not for themselves but for God and his Christ - for the God-man who lived and died for all the world; men and women who cannot even conceive of love of God which does not include love for the least of their neighbors; *men and women completely convinced that love of God which does not issue in justice for others is a farce.* (Emphasis mine)

This week, each of us needs to ask ourselves a question- do we live for Christ or for the world? Are we men and women for others? May Christ Jesus and He alone reign in our hearts, our minds, and our souls! Saint Ignatius Loyola, help us set the world on fire with the love of Christ, our King. Saint Ignatius Loyola, help us to become standard bearers for the Kingdom of Christ!

Twenty-Sixth Sunday in Ordinary Time

The Lord Jesus, in today's Gospel given to us from the Evangelist Saint Luke, tells us a very interesting parable, one about the rich man, Dives, and the poor man, Lazarus. We should note that the Lazarus of this parable is not the same Lazarus about whom we read in John's Gospel, the dear friend of the Lord Jesus, the brother of Mary and Martha, but merely a character in this powerful parable. And, it should also be noted that, if we read the story, the rich man in the parable is not ascribed a name. The name "Dives" which he is sometimes called is really just the Latin Word meaning "rich man."

The story of Lazarus, who spends his days outside the house of a rich man, begging and ill, so infirm that he could not even stop the dogs from coming over and licking his sores, and Dives, a wealthy man, can teach us many things. First, it can teach us that, in the end, we are all the same; second, it can teach us that some people, no matter what, will not change; and third, it can teach us that there are very real, very eternal consequences for we live our life here on earth.

First, this parable of Lazarus and Dive can teach us that, in the end, we are all the same. Look at Dives, with his fine food, comfortable clothes, and extravagant lifestyle. He was in the lap of luxury in this life. Look at Lazarus, a poor, sick, beggar. He was in torment in his life, so downtrodden was he in his life. And, in the final moments, death came for both of them. Both were mortal men and both one day met their maker. Dives could take none of his possessions with him to the netherworld; and in the justice that is Christ, Lazarus rests comfortable in the bosom of Abraham, our father in faith.

Like it or not, death stops for each and every one of us. I don't mean to a be a downer, but none of us will live forever. This is a reality of our fallen human condition, one that has, as a consequence of our fall in original sin, death. We come into this world with nothing and we leave with nothing.

Second, this parable of Lazarus and Dives can teach us that some people, no matter what, will not really change. And, despite our best efforts, we can't force people to change. The old adage, " a leopard can't change his spots" isn't exactly true because there is always the opportunity for repentance and change, as long as we can take a living breath. But sometimes people simply won't change. Even in death, Dives is still trying to get what he wants done, trying to get others to do what he wants when he wants it. Even in the netherworld, he still is trying to have Lazarus go and warn his brothers of the fate that waits for them if they do not repent. "Send Lazarus…" "Tell Lazarus to dip his finger…" Apologies without a change of behavior is merely insincere manipulation.

Third, this parable of Lazarus and Dives can teach us that there are very real, very eternal consequences for how we live our lives here in this life. We need to be aware of the four last things of our faith: death, judgment, Heaven, and hell. By living or by not living our lives in accordance with the commandments, by being or by not being women and men of mercy and justice, we determine our eternal fate. *The Catechism of the Catholic Church* (1035) tells us: "The teaching of the Church affirms the existence of hell and its eternity. Immediately after death the souls of those who die in a state of mortal sin descend into hell, where they suffer the punishments of hell, 'eternal fire.' The chief punishment of hell is eternal separation from

God, in whom alone man can possess the life and happiness for which he was created and for which he longs."

Yes, this parable of Lazarus and Dives is one from which we can learn many lessons. Pray this week for the grace to appreciate the gifts of God given to us in this life so that we can be with him in the next.

Twenty-Seventh Sunday in Ordinary Time

In the Gospel that we proclaim this morning from the Evangelist Luke, there is the intrinsic connection made between humility and faith. In fact, it can be said that humility is the basis of faith.

Let's start at the beginning, with our first parents, Adam and Eve, about whom we read in the Book of Genesis. Did they have faith? Did they need faith? After all, they, living in original innocence, spoke with God. Scripture tells us that they walked with God in the cool of the night. Adam and Eve knew God. I'd like to think that they were familiar with God, perhaps too familiar. God creates them in his image and likeness and they are fundamentally good. God grants them everything they need.

God requires only one thing: Adam and Eve cannot eat of the fruit of the tree of the knowledge of good and evil. And who enters the picture? The evil one, Satan, who plays on the basic insecurity that is man: "Eat of the fruit of this tree and you will be more than God."

So, what exactly is original sin? We read in the Catechism that original sin is, ultimately, lack of trust in the Creator and abuse of the great gift of free will given to us from God our Father (CCC 397).

In this sin of choosing to disobey the one thing that the Creator had asked our first parents to do, namely not to eat of the fruit of the tree of the knowledge of good and evil, Adam and Eve forget their place in the universe. They forgot that God is Creator and that they are creatures. They who were called to be "like God" suddenly decided that they wanted to be "without God, before God and not in accordance with God" (CCC 398).

They who were created in the image and likeness of God began to reflect a distorted likeness (CCC 400), almost as in a funhouse mirror. Everything is put into disarray, and all relationships are thrown asunder.

In human relationships, the human being is divided in himself and in his thoughts. He knows in the deepest part of his soul that he is created to know, serve and love God in this life and to be with Him in the next. But if he's honest, he knows he really wants to serve himself first. His focus is on the things of this world, not on his true home, Heaven. The human being's relationship with the world is now disordered.

As the Catechism reminds us, "visible creation has become alien and hostile to man," and relationships with fellow humans has become difficult. Even the most primordial relationship, that of man and woman, is "subject to tensions, their relations henceforth marked by lust and domination." (CCC 400). We see the bad fruits of sin: a three-fold alienation of the human being from God, others and self. And we see the true wages of sin: death. And because of this lack of humility, Adam and Eve fail to recognize God. They do not trust God and because of this, they lack faith.

In other words, we recognize the fact that God is God, that we are not God, and thank God for that! Be content with who and what we are- beloved children of God, redeemed by the blood of his Son, our Lord, Jesus Christ.

Twenty-Eighth Sunday in Ordinary Time

The character of Han Solo has been portrayed by Harrison Ford since the very first film set in a galaxy, far, far away, namely *Star Wars: A New Hope* in 1977. Ford's Han Solo was known as a tough guy, a rogue and a scoundrel, but with a heart of gold. He was known in the films to be a skeptic when it came to the "Force," the animating force in the "Star Wars Universe," which controls all things, and which Jedi (the good guys, if you will) and the Sith (the very bad guys) can tap into and use for heroics or villainy.

In one telling scene in that first film in the franchise, Solo states the following to the young and idealistic main hero of the movie, Luke Skywalker (played by Mark Hamill):

Han Solo: *Hokey religions and ancient weapons are no match for a good blaster at your side, kid.*

Luke Skywalker: *You don't believe in the Force, do you?*

Han Solo: *Kid, I've flown from one side of this galaxy to the other. I've seen a lot of strange stuff, but I've never seen anything to make me believe there's one all-powerful force controlling everything. There's no mystical energy field that controls my destiny.*

Many years later, the seventh film in the Star Wars story was released in 2015, entitled *Star Wars: The Force Awakens* (2015). In one scene in the 2015 film, the older Han Solo, now a father whose son is turning into a bad guy (spoilers are allowed since the film has been out for a while now), turns and states "(t)he crazy thing is it's all true…the force, the Jedi…it's all true."

The same can be said for each and every aspect of our Catholic faith. The things we as Catholic Christians believe are all true. They are all true and then all logically follow, if we take the time to think and to understand what it is that the Church teaches and what we profess in the Creed. And one of those truths is the final judgement of Christ the King, who as we profess in the Creed, will come again in glory to judge the living and the death.

The Gospel parable given to us from Saint John teaches us that sin is very real, and that judgement will come to those who reject the heir, the Son, Jesus Christ, our Lord, the son of the Eternal Father.

It is important to place our thoughts especially in this time of year when the light is growing lesser, the temperature is growing colder, and even nature itself seems to be shedding its last bursts of growth in the form of leaves falling from the trees this autumn. Winter is coming, that cold, that dark, and yet somehow hopeful season of the calendar year.

In our Church's liturgical calendar, we have almost reached once again the end of our Church's liturgical year. We put our focus on the realities, both natural and supernatural, of which many of us would rather not face, namely our own earthly demise and what happens next.

The truth is there. One day, the Lord Jesus Christ, the merciful one, will come again. This Lord of love and mercy is also a God of justice and he will judge the living and the dead, each person according to one key question, as the Spanish mystic Saint John of the Cross asks: "How have you loved?"

Yes, it is all true, including the fact of what is called *i Novissimi* (the four last things), namely death, judgement, Heaven, and hell. One day, as we read about in today's Gospel, when the appointed time has come, Jesus Christ will come again in glory to judge the living and the death and every single soul will have to account for his or her actions and inactions, all of our unconfessed, unrepented sins. Christ will come at the end of time for the final judgment s.

Heaven is real. Purgatory is real. And yes, hell is also real. We have a God who loves us enough to become one like us in all things, but sin. We have a God who opens his arms wide on the cross in an embrace of love for you and for me. We have a God who is rich in mercy and who possesses a universal salvific will and yes, we can dare to hope that all will be saved.

However, we have a God who is justice. God wants to save all, but that means that we have to do some work. There are moral implications for every single thing that we do. Remember, God does not send anyone to hell. We send ourselves there by our own inability to love, to forgive, to ask for forgiveness. The Church has said that there are plenty of people in Heaven- we call them the Saints! But she has never dogmatically said that any soul is in hell. But since we have free will, no doubt that there are some there. *The Catechism of the Catholic Church* (1035-1037) teaches us the following:

The chief punishment of hell is eternal separation from God, in whom alone man can possess the life and happiness for which he was created and for which he longs. The affirmations of Sacred Scripture and the teachings of the Church on the subject of hell are a call to the responsibility incumbent upon man to make use of his freedom in view of his eternal

destiny. They are at the same time an urgent call to conversion: "Enter by the narrow gate; for the gate is wide and the
way is easy, that leads to destruction, and those who enter by
it are many. For the gate is narrow and the way is hard, that
leads to life, and those who find it are few." Since we know
neither the day nor the hour, we should follow the advice of
the Lord and watch constantly so that, when the single
course of our earthly life is completed, we may merit to enter
with him into the marriage feast and be numbered among
the blessed, and not, like the wicked and slothful servants, be
ordered to depart into the eternal fire, into the outer darkness where "men will weep and gnash their teeth." God pre-
destines no one to go to hell; for this, a willful turning away
from God (a mortal sin) is necessary, and persistence in it
until the end. In the Eucharistic liturgy and in the daily prayers of her faithful, the Church implores the mercy of God,
who does not want "any to perish, but all to come to repentance."

Saint John of the Cross wrote: "In the evening of life, we will be
judged on love alone." How we love and how serve God and our
neighbor will determine our place in the afterlife. Are we aiming to
spend the afterlife in our true homeland, Heaven, or are we content
to just make it to Purgatory. Remember, all of it, Heaven, Purgatory,
and, yes, hell, are all very, very real. We are pilgrims on this earthly
plane and it is our task to return to our heavenly homeland.

Twenty-Ninth Sunday in Ordinary Time

I don't need to tell you that we live in a fallen world, a world that is still groaning under the effects of the original sin of our first parents, Adam and Eve. Yes, that sin of hubris, of pride, of failure to remember that God is God, that we are not God, and thank God for that, affects humanity to this day. Yes, through the great and powerful sacrament of Baptism, we as Christians are incorporated into the Mystical Body of Christ, with all of sins washed away. We are made clean. And yet, the marks of concupiscence are still around us, the inclination to want to always take the easy way out, the desire to do the wrong thing, even when we know it's the wrong thing, the inclination to always surrender to the flesh, that's still around and it's still in us.

Through the disobedience of one man, Adam, we have inherited death. Through the obedience, the supreme filial obedience of Christ the Lord, the new Adam, we have inherited new and eternal life. What should our response be? Perhaps we might offer a three-fold response:

First, recognize that the world is fallen. There are a lot of "unjust judges," those who, unfortunately, really aren't that concerned for our welfare, but are more concerned for their own welfare. We can't be naïve. The time to view the world through "rose-colored glasses" has long since ceased. There's some really bad stuff out there and we are being inundated with it constantly, much especially through the media. I don't need to enumerate the ways in which the world is fallen. Many of you know it far, far better than me and it serves no purpose for me a homilist to bemoan the state of the world.

Second, recognize that, even though the world is fallen, it is redeemed. Yes, this world of ours which tramples constantly and continually on human life, which shows no value to the lives of the unborn, the differently abled, the poor, and the migrant, this world which demonstrates continual distain for the lives of the elderly and the ill, is redeemed in the one, single sacrifice of Christ Jesus on the Cross, It is the red rain that is his most precious blood which washes over us, cleansing us, and for the sake of his sorrowful passion, allows God the Eternal Father to have mercy on us and on the whole world.

Third and finally, recognize that all we need to do in this fallen, yet redeemed world, is to trust in the words offered by Our Blessed Lord in the Gospel of Saint Luke today:

"Will not God then secure the rights of his chosen ones
who call out to him day and night?
Will he be slow to answer them?
I tell you, he will see to it that justice is done for them speedily."

We as Christians are called to perseverance in our struggle, to be like that widow who is berating the unjust judge for a fair response. We can't give up searching and striving for good. And, at the same time, we need to trust the fact that God has already won the battle. He is the victor and, although we only know it dimly now, we share in his triumph.

The Lord Jesus ends today with a pointed question: "When the Son of Man comes, do you think that he will find faith in the world?" Please God, through our trust and perseverance, our loving Christ will find this to be true in us.

Thirtieth Sunday in Ordinary Time

In 1993, when I was a college-level seminarian, I attended a production at Radio City Music Hall on the life of Our Blessed Lord, Jesus. I attended with the other college seminarians of the now-defunct seminary house of formation in Douglaston, Queens and even as a twenty-year-old, I was rather underwhelmed. I remember being particularly disturbed, and, indeed perplexed, by this particular production's portrayal of the Pharisees.

What did the Pharisees look like in this show? Well, to be honest, all they were missing were the twirling mustaches and black top hats, a 1990s "Snidely Whiplash," as if they would tie fair maidens to the railroad tracks and we, the audience, would hope against hope that the brave hero would rescue the poor girl! What made this portrayal over-the-top for me was the fact that the Pharisees dressed in black and had quasi-Darth Vader from *Star Wars* helmets. It was all too much to me.

From that time onward, I promised that I would not look at the Pharisees, the Sadducees, and the other religious groups with whom Our Blessed Lord Jesus had come into conflict, on a one- dimensional level. I wanted to know more about these groups from biblical history so that I could grow to dislike them without their "Darth Vader" helmets.

From my studies, I found myself quite disappointed. In fact, I actually grew to sympathize with the Pharisees. In fact, I even came to the realization that, if I were alive during the earthly life of Our Blessed Lord Jesus, perhaps I might have even been sympathetic to these now reviled figures in the New Testament. Maybe I even might have been one of them.

So, with this in mind, let's examine exactly who the Pharisees were. Well, for starters, they were part of a reform movement. These men had the biggest influence on the interpretation of the Law at the time of Our Blessed Lord Jesus. Historically, the Pharisees came about in the second century B.C. Their name meant the "pious" and their main idea was to keep to the purity of the Jewish faith against the growing threat of the culture of the Greek influenced world of the day, which was called Hellenism.

The main goal of the Pharisees was to see that every aspect of life is holy. They wanted to appeal in their interpretation of their religion only to the written text. They were called the *p'rushim*, the "separated ones," and they wanted to avoid anything that would render themselves impure. They followed laws and observances that went far beyond what the average Jew would do, following prescriptions of the law that would have only been observed by Jewish priests.

As I learned this about the Pharisees, I began to see that perhaps I would have been one of them. I want to be a holy, pious, observant follower of the law of the Lord. I want to be holy in following the laws, the rubrics, the official documents of the Church, which I have studied and which I teach to the seminarians with whom I am blessed to minister.

So, if this is the case, perhaps the Pharisees weren't mustache-twirling bad guys. But why were they wrong? May I suggest this one reason: these good men put their faith in the letter of the Law strictly, and, in doing so, they could not see that the Law had been fulfilled in the midst in the Divine Person of Our Blessed Lord Jesus. The Law and the way to holiness is not found in propositional rules, even though the rules we follow in our faith are good (and, indeed, essential), but in a Person, a Divine Person in two natures, Christ Jesus Our Lord.

Every rule, every observance of the Lord is important and we can recall that Our Blessed Lord Jesus stated that he has come not to change a single iota of the Law, but to fulfill the Law. The Lord Jesus Christ is not just the bringer of the Law, the New Covenant, but he is the Law. He is the Law and the Lawgiver, he is the messenger and the message, he is the teacher and he is what is taught. Yes, Jesus Christ is, in his very Person, the Kingdom of God.

Therefore, for us as contemporary Catholics, we need to recall that we are not following a set of laws (as important as regulations are for us as Catholics). We are not just following a moral code. Our faith is in God Incarnate, the God-Man Christ Jesus, our Lord, our God, our Savior, he who through the miracle of the Incarnation, the taking on of flesh of the Second Person of the Most Blessed Trinity, is truly Emmanuel, God-with-us. Our faith is not in a system of laws, but in he who is the fulfillment of the Laws.

This leads us to the other problem with the Pharisees. As I had mentioned, they were known as the *p'rushim*, the "separated ones. Would it be better for us as Catholic Christians to separate ourselves from society, to see the world as evil, and to try to break away? Is something like what Rod Dreher called for in his very influential text, *The Benedict Option* (2016), what we should do, namely to separate as Christians from the wicked world and make small groups wherein we can promote and defend the Christian faith?

I would say that this is not the message of the Gospel and is completely foreign to the Gospel. Our Blessed Lord said to his disciples to go and to preach all nations, not to become that light hidden under the basket or to bury our talent, so as to keep it safe against the capriciousness and cruelty of the world. We as Christians are called to be in the world, and yet, not of the world. We have to be in dialogue with the world while, at the same time, never marry the spirit of the present age, because, if we do so, we as Mother Church will wind up a young widow.

When we look to the Pharisees, we should not see monsters, but perhaps see genuinely good men who missed the mark. They could not the Messiah standing in their midst. I know that I have been like them. Perhaps you might have been as well. Please pray for the grace this week to avoid this "leaven."

Thirty-First Sunday in Ordinary Time

The Gospel we proclaim this Sunday features a rather enigmatic figure, one whom we read about only in this Gospel passage: Zacchaeus. What can we learn from this story of this "short-in-stature" man, a chief tax collector, a man who changes his life, who climbs a sycamore tree because he was "seeking to see who Jesus was?" I think that we can learn two powerful lessons. First, Christ desires our salvation, giving us again and again chances to come to him, to learn from him, to know him as our Lord and Savior. Second, what are we willing to do to see this Jesus, this one whom we have come to know as our friend, our brother, our loving redeemer? What are we willing to risk?

First, do we recognize that Our Lord Jesus wants our salvation? Jesus knows us, inside and out. He knows our faults and failings, he knows our sins. He knows all the bad that we have done; he knows all the bad intentions of our wills. He has seen us in our ugliness, in our brokenness, and still, he loves us. Yes, Jesus, he who is the Word Incarnate, the Second Person of the Most Blessed Trinity, he who is in his very Person God Almighty, the Savior of all mankind, deeply, truly, madly loves us. Yes, God knows us inside and out and still he loves us.

This Jesus loves us! He opens his arms on the Cross in an embrace of love and in the red rain that is his Precious Blood washes us clean! The Lord wants one thing: our salvation. That is his very nature. Jesus' name means "God Saves" in Hebrew. What does this tell us about Jesus? It means that it is he who was sent to save us from our sins. The title "Christ" is Greek for "anointed one" or "Messiah."

So, if we were to put the name of the Lord Jesus together with the title or adjective most properly and most commonly given to him, we could see that he is Jesus Christ, or "the Messiah who saves!" In theological terms, we call the study of who Jesus is "Christology" and we call the study of what he does as "Soteriology," namely the study of how Jesus who is God saves us. When we say the name, Jesus Christ, we are making a statement of faith! When we say the name, Jesus Christ, we learn all we need to know about Jesus. It is in who he is to save us!

Second, little Zacchaeus, a man of wealth, a man of means, is willing to embarrass himself, climbing the sycamore tree to see the Lord Jesus, to view this man about whom he has heard so much. He is willing to "go out on a limb," risking his pride, risking his reputation, to see Jesus. Granted, Zacchaeus is a man who, as a tax collector, is not respected by his own Jewish community. He is considered to be a cheat, thought to be a collaborator with the oppressors, the Romans. But, in reality, Zacchaeus probably was living a rather comfortable life. He has all he needs. And with all this in mind, this little man shows great spirit to risk his way of life to see and follow the Lord.

What are we willing to risk to follow the Lord? It is a dangerous thing to posit belief in a God whom we cannot see. It is a scary thing to live our lives in accordance with the teachings of a man who lived over 2,000 years ago. What if we're wrong? What if we spend our entire lives trying to live good lives of service and love and ultimately find out that there is nothing else, that we could have done whatever we wanted, even the most immoral of activities?

The question needs to be asked: Do I believe, really truly, deeply believe that there really is a God? Do I believe that this God has revealed Himself to the world in the Person of Christ? Do I really believe that the Lord Jesus' life continues on today in His Body, the Church? Am I willing to risk it, putting aside my fear and uncertainty to follow Christ?

This fear can exist not only in questions of the existence of God, the revelation of Christ and the necessity of the Church in general but can also be extended to our own lives. If God exists, why should He love me with all my faults, with all my sins, with all my problems and anxieties?

This fear and doubt can extend to our life choices. We can doubt ourselves in our relationships with others – being afraid to let others into our lives, being afraid to love, to be loved and to be vulnerable. Every time we open our mouths, we are being judged. What if the person with whom I share my thoughts betrays me, mocks me or misunderstands me? Am I worthy of the friendship that is offered to me by another? Am I lovable?

Overcoming the fear that exists in us is essential for our lives of faith. The only way to do so is to keep on going, gazing intently on Jesus – the way, the truth and the life for us. If we trust in him who cannot deceive or be deceived, if we are open to his healing and trust in the plan that he has for our lives, we will know his healing and his peace. This week, be like Zacchaeus! Don't be afraid to go out on a limb to see Jesus who loves us and who desires nothing more than to save us!

Thirty-Second Sunday in Ordinary Time

In the first reading we proclaim today from the Second Book of Maccabees, a mother encourages her seven sons to remain faithful to the law of the Lord. One of the brothers proclaims: "We are ready to die rather than transgress the laws of our ancestors."

All the brothers have to do is to violate their consciences, to eat pork in contradiction to the Old Covenant. What would you do? The American Catholic writer Flannery O'Connor commented: "When you can assume that your audience holds the same beliefs you do, you can relax a little and use more normal ways of talking to it; when you have to assume that it does not, then you have to make your vision apparent by shock — to the hard of hearing you shout, and for the almost blind you draw large and startling figures." The world, by and large, doesn't hold the same beliefs as you and I do. It doesn't speak the same language as the Christian does.

In Rome, the Basilica of San Stefano on the Caelian Hill is filled with frescoes painted by the artists Pomarancio and Tempesta. The paintings are brutal and grotesque, and they are disturbing, but life can be brutal, too, especially life in our world today.

The images are meant to wake us up from our slumber to the reality of what the world is for Christians.

The frescoes serve a powerful purpose: to scream at us Christians, urging us to wake up. The martyrs depicted here are meant to inspire courage in our hearts, imploring those who are able to do so to perceive beyond the values set by this world, begging us to grow in an openness to the supernatural in our all too natural, fallen world.

Martyrs speak to us. These martyrs make the faith credible. They are the ultimate expression of the credibility of Divine Revelation. That was true in the Maccabees' time and in the time of the martyrs depicted in that Roman basilica, and it is true in the present.

To give a modern example, when ISIS savagely murdered 20 Egyptian men and one Ghanaian man in January 2015, and then released the video a month later, stating that "Rome is next," their plan backfired, because the 20 Coptic Christians and one Muslim who were killed became inspirations.

The Muslim man, Matthew Ayariga, was, by his actions, baptized in blood, convinced of the truth of the Christian faith because of the witness of his fellow workers. "Their God is my God. I will go with them," he uttered, even when he could have been pardoned by his executioners.

This reading challenges us at the very core of our system of values. It challenges us and asks us a vital question: As Christians, as those incorporated into the Body of Christ, the church, are we in the world or of the world?

If we are to be Christian in the world today, we will suffer daily martyrdoms. The Lord Jesus, the King of Martyrs suffered, and so will we. Most likely, our martyrdoms will not be physical, but subtler, and we see that played out in the last acceptable prejudice, anti-Catholicism, in a generally secular society.

When someone stands for objective truth and natural law in the age of subjective reality, he or she is called a bigot. If we stand true in every aspect of our faith, we will suffer. The fourth brother in the first reading states: "It is my choice to die at the hands of men with the hope God gives of being raised up by him; but for you, there will be no resurrection to life."

Have faith and follow Christ. If we are faithful to Him, He will remain faithful to us. The ultimate credibility of the faith is martyrdom. Have faith that the Lord will support us, even in the martyrdoms of daily life.

Feast of the Dedication of the Lateran Cathedral

Growing up as a kid in Park Slope, Brooklyn, I literally did not know anyone that was not a Roman Catholic and who wasn't either of Irish descent. Sure, I knew that other people existed, in theory- I mean, I'd seen them on television or in the streets; I just didn't know any of them personally!

The world where I lived, well, it was rather small and insular, despite coming from New York City, considered by some to be the crossroads of the world. It wasn't until high school that I got to know people who weren't either Irish. It wasn't until college that I got to know people who weren't Catholic.

We as Catholics can be a lot like that, too, for some reason. Simply because of the structure of our church, we can forget how big we really are. If you grew up in certain parts of the country, like in New York or Boston or Philadelphia, you could find a Catholic Church every other block. The good thing about the parish system is that it promoted strong Catholic identity; the bad thing was that often one parish was considered to be like a foreign land compared to its neighbor.

Today's feast, the dedication of the Basilica of St. John Lateran, the mother church of all Christianity, serves to remind us that our faith is more than just our own personal business; it's more than just our own parish; it's more than just our local dioceses; it's more than even the national church in our country; we are part of a Church that bears the four marks of the Church- one, holy, catholic, and apostolic. We are founded by Christ, on the rock that is Peter and the Apostles. We as a Church are more than just the Church that we see here on earth; we, as the Church universal, are part of the Church militant, comprising Christians on earth who are living; Christian militia, who struggle against sin, the devil and "..the rulers of the darkness of this world, against spiritual wickedness in high places" as Ephesians 6:12 tells us; but there is also the Church Triumphant (*Ecclesia Triumphans*), comprising those who are in Heaven, and the Church Penitent (*Ecclesia Penitens*), a.k.a. *Church Suffering* or *Church Padecent* or Church Expectant (*Ecclesia Expectans*), which in Catholic theology comprises those Christians presently in Purgatory.

We celebrate this feast because it reminds us to think big, not small, when it comes to the Church. True, we are part of history, and it is that incarnational moment that is the center of our Church and our salvation. We are founded as a Church in a particular place and time. Listen to the words of the great Catholic thinker, Hilaire Belloc:

> *Every manifestation of divine influence among men must have its human circumstance of place and time. The Church might have risen under Divine Providence in any spot; it did, as a fact, spring up in the high Greek tide of the Levant and carries to this day the noble Hellenic garb. It might have risen at any time; it did, as a fact, rise just at the inception of that united Imperial Roman system which we are about to examine. It might have carried for its ornaments and have had for its sacred language the accoutrements and the speech of any one of the other great civilizations, living or dead: of Assyria, of Egypt, of Persia, of China, of the Indies. As a matter of*

historical fact, the Church was so circumstanced in its origin and development that its external accoutrement and its language were those of the Mediterranean, that is, of Greece and Rome: of the Empire.

But our Church is so much more than this: it involves everyone, in all places and in all time. As another author, James Joyce, declares: "Here comes everybody." Indeed, in celebrating today the feast of the dedication of the Papal Cathedral, the Patriarchal Basilica of Saint John Lateran, this is the celebration of the Catholic Church, east and west, in heaven, on earth, and in purgatory. Today is the celebration of our foundation by Christ on the Rock that is Peter, now known as Francis. May zeal for our house always consume us.

Thirty-Third Sunday in Ordinary Time

Emily Dickinson, in her poem numbered 479, more commonly known by the first line of the work, "Because I could not stop for death," writes:

Because I could not stop for Death,
He kindly stopped for me;
The Carriage held but just Ourselves
And Immortality.
We slowly drove, He knew no haste
And I had put away
My labor and my leisure too,
For His Civility.
We passed the School, where
Children strove
At Recess, in the Ring,
We passed the Fields of Gazing Grain,
We passed the Setting Sun,
Or rather, He passed Us.
The Dews drew quivering and Chill
For only Gossamer, my Gown,
My Tippet, only Tulle,
We paused before a House that seemed
A Swelling of the Ground.
The Roof was scarcely visible,
The Cornice, in the Ground,
Since then, 'tis Centuries, and yet

Feels shorter than the Day
I first surmised the Horses' Heads
Were toward Eternity.

The poet is correct. The truth is that with each day, I am passing away and so is everyone else, just like everyone before us did. In today's Gospel from Luke, we hear the story of the Final Judgment. All of us, no matter who we are, will face the end. But the even greater truth is that death is not the end. It is not, as Shakespeare calls it in Act 3 of "Hamlet," the "unknown country," but something we know by faith, something that we grasp, as the Apostle Paul tells us, "hoping against hope."

This month of November is the month of the Holy Souls. It is a beautiful month, one that makes us stop to take account of where we are and where we are going.

Through faith and through our incorporation into the Body of Christ by baptism, we have the assurance that all those whom we have loved and lost, all those whom we love and cherish here on earth, will, please God, be united around the heavenly throne one day.

This month of the Holy Souls teaches us two lessons: First, we need to understand and to embrace our own mortality, and second, we as Christians have an obligation to pray for the dead.

First, there is the very real need for "memento mori" — to remember that we are all passing away. The Franciscan Capuchin Crypt near Piazza Barberini in Rome teaches us that lesson, as does the Capela dos Ossas in Portugal, whose inscription over the chapel's door reads: "We bones that here are, for yours await."

I have seen the grave in which one day I will rest in Brooklyn's Greenwood Cemetery. Every day, we come a little bit closer to it.

Second, we shouldn't neglect those who have gone before us; we need to pray for them, the poor souls in purgatory, for where they are, we will be, hoping for the eternal light to be shown to us. It is a spiritual work of mercy. A simple prayer we can say for the dead this month and indeed every day is, "Eternal rest grant unto them, O Lord, and let perpetual light shine upon them. May the souls of the faithful departed, through the mercy of God, rest in peace. Amen."

One resolution, then, in light of this fact of our faith is to live each day as if it were our last, cherishing in and relishing in the gift of our lives in this plane of reality.

Also, remember that the people in our lives are far too precious to neglect. And, finally remember what really matters in the end are three things — faith, hope and love. That's what lasts.

The Solemnity of Jesus Christ, King of the Universe

With this solemnity of the Our Lord Jesus Christ, King of the Universe, we come on this Sunday to the end of the Year of Grace. In order to understand this great feast, we need to put it into the proper context.

Pope Pius XI instituted the solemnity in reaction to the state of the world after the First World War, the "war to end all wars." The war had seen the end of the reigns of many of the noble families of Europe and Asia from Russia to Turkey to Germany to Austria, and even Great Britain, on whose empire "the sun never sets," was beginning to show the cracks in the foundation that would visibly crumble after the Second World War.

Communism as seen in Stalin and fascism as demonstrated by Mussolini and other radical ideologies were rising throughout the world. Nazism was just around the corner. And soon, the United States would experience the Great Depression.

The Vatican itself would soon lose more temporal power with the Lateran Treaty. The world as it was known was suddenly changing. Who was in charge?

Pope Pius XI, in an earlier encyclical, *Ubi arcano*, recognized this reality: "...manifold evils in the world were due to the fact that the majority of men had thrust Jesus Christ and his holy law out of their lives; that these had no place either in private affairs or in politics: and we said further, that as long as individuals and states refused to submit to the rule of our Savior, there would be no really hopeful prospect of a lasting peace among nations."

Who is in charge? Ultimately, it is Christ who reigns. Pope Pius XI, in 1925 in his encyclical, *Quas primas*, wrote: "He is said to reign 'in the hearts of men,' both by reason of the keenness of his intellect and the extent of his knowledge, and also because he is very truth, and it is from him that truth must be obediently received by all mankind ... He is King of hearts, too, by reason of his 'charity which exceedeth all knowledge'."

So, a question for us then, as we examine our lives, our souls, our consciences, at the conclusion of this Year of Grace and prepare next Sunday to begin a new liturgical year with the First Sunday of Advent: Have we allowed Our Lord Jesus Christ to be king of our hearts, our minds, our wills, indeed our very soul?

As Christians, we are incorporated into the Mystical Body of Christ, and as such, we have to make decisions, for Christ and his church or against Christ and his church.

St. Ignatius Loyola, the founder of the Jesuits, in his Spiritual Exercises speaks of "The Two Standards:" the way of the Lord Jesus or the way of the world. By his use of the term, "standard," St. Ignatius means a banner under which a regiment marches. We as Christians have to make a choice. And what better day to make that choice than on this feast of Our Lord Jesus, Christ King of the Universe.

Once we choose God over mammon, once we pick the things of the Lord over the things of his world, the haze of self-deception is lifted. And as Christ did, we recognize that we live not for ourselves, but for Christ and for others. Our response to the gratuitous gift of God that is our very existence is not a concern for "What's in it for me"? but a call to see God in all things. Having become able to see Christ in all things, we then recognize that we are to be the heart, the hands and the voice of Christ in the world, especially to the poor, the weak, the forgotten and the oppressed. This is our task of servitude to Christ, our King.

Thanksgiving Day (U.S.A.)

This Gospel that we proclaim today is the very famous story of the ten lepers. This Gospel is used to indicate that we should have a true spirit of thanksgiving, but it has, in fact, a deeper Christological meaning.

Jesus is the Master Teacher and everything that he does, all of his words and gestures have great significance. Everything that Jesus says and everything that he does points to who he is- the Christ of God. Jesus reveals in every moment of his life his mission, which is also who he is in himself.

Note careful the Lord Jesus' instructions in this Gospel. What does the Lord Jesus order the lepers to do? "Go and show yourself to the priest." Who is the one who returns to say thank you? It is the Samaritan.

On the human level, due to societal norms, the leper cannot go and show himself to the priest. He is a Samaritan, part of a community whom Jewish priests of Jesus' day believed to be racial and religious traitors. Simply put, a priest would not welcome the leper. Yet, in fact, it is this that the Samaritan leper precisely does- the thankful Samaritan leper shows himself to THE PRIEST- the one and only true High Priest, Christ the Lord.

Going further with the concept of Christ's absolute divinity, we have today's Gospel- this one and true High Priest IS in fact the long-awaited Kingdom of God. It is the Lord Jesus who is the messenger and the message, the teacher and that what is taught. The Lord Jesus Himself is the Kingdom of God.

In today's Gospel, the Lord reminds us not to go searching for the Kingdom of God, not to go run off in pursuit of the Kingdom of God. He is already in our midst, just like he was for the leper, right in our midst, breaking in, "already, but not yet" fully present in our world. In our midst, most especially in his Eucharistic self, we have the true High Priest. In his Body and Blood found present in the Eucharist, we have the Kingdom of God. So, I say to you today- "look, there he is." Give thanks that you and I can go show ourselves to the priest.

About the Author

Father John P. Cush, STD, a priest of the Diocese of Brooklyn, is the Editor-in-Chief of Homiletic and Pastoral Review. Fr. Cush serves as a full-time Professor of Dogmatic and Fundamental Theology, Director of Seminarian Admissions and Recruitment, and Formation Advisor at Saint Joseph's Seminary and College in New York. Before that, he served in parochial work and in full-time high school teaching in the Diocese of Brooklyn and had served as Academic Dean/Assistant Vice-Rector and Formation Advisor at the Pontifical North American College Rome, Italy. Fr. Cush has taught theology and Church History at the Pontifical Gregorian University, the Pontifical University of Saint Thomas Aquinas (the Angelicum), and the Pontifical University of the Holy Cross (Santa Croce), all in Rome, Italy.

Fr. Cush holds the pontifical doctorate in sacred theology (STD) from the Pontifical Gregorian University, Rome, Italy in the field of fundamental theology, He had also studied dogmatic theology at the Pontifical University of Saint Thomas Aquinas (the Angelicum), Rome, Italy, on the graduate level. Fr. Cush is the author of *The How-to-Book of Theology* (OSV Press, 2020) and *Theology as Prayer: a Primer for Diocesan Priests* (with Msgr. Walter Oxley), as well as being a contributor to the festschrift *Intellect, Affect, and God* (Marquette University Press, 2021). He is also the author of *Nothing But You: Reflections on the Priesthood and Priestly Formation through the Lens of Bishop Robert Barron* (Word on Fire, July 2024).